PHILIP'S Red Books

LOCAL STREET ATLAS

CRAWLEY
MID-SUSSEX

BURGESS HILL · EAST GRINSTEAD · GATWICK
HAYWARDS HEATH · HORLEY · HORSHAM

ONLY £3.75

Including:

- Area Road Map
- Hospitals
- Car Parks
- Post Offices
- One-Way Streets
- Leisure Facilities
- Industrial Areas
- Retail Areas
- Index with Postcodes

14th Edition

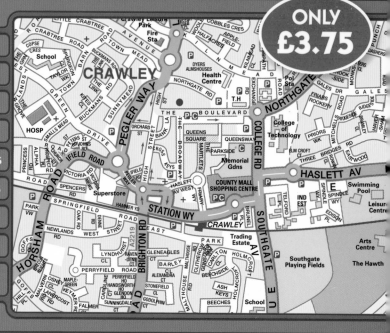

Scale - 4 Inches to 1 Mile

Enlarged Centre for: **CRAWLEY**

PHILIP'S *Red Books* showing the way

LOCAL STREET ATLAS

CRAWLEY MID-SUSSEX

BURGESS HILL · EAST GRINSTEAD · GATWICK
HAYWARDS HEATH · HORLEY · HORSHAM

CONTENTS

Page Layout & Road Map......................2
4 Miles to 1 Inch

Crawley Enlarged Centre 3
7 Inches to 1 Mile

Street Maps.................................. 4-38
4 Inches to 1 Mile

Index to Streets................................38

www.philips-maps.co.uk

First published in 2005 by
Estate Publications

This edition published by Philip's,
a division of Octopus Publishing Group Ltd
www.octopusbooks.co.uk
2–4 Heron Quays, London E14 4JP
An Hachette Livre UK Company

Second impression 2008
14/01-05

ISBN 978-0-540-09355-7

© Philip's 2008

This product includes mapping data licensed
from Ordnance Survey®, with the permission
of the Controller of Her Majesty's Stationery
Office.© Crown copyright 2005. All rights
reserved. Licence number 100011710

LEGEND

Symbol	Description
	Motorway
	Primary Route
	Other 'A' Road
	'B' Road
	Minor Road
	Pedestrianized / Restricted Access
	Track
	Built Up Area
	Footpath
	Stream
	River
Lock	Canal
	Railway / Station
●	Post Office
P P+	Car Park / Park & Ride
C	Public Convenience
+	Place of Worship
→	One-way Street
i	Tourist Information Centre
8 8	Adjoining Pages
	Area Depicting Enlarged Centre
	Emergency Services
	Industrial Buildings
	Leisure Buildings
	Education Buildings
	Hotels etc.
	Retail Buildings
	General Buildings
	Woodland
	Orchard
	Recreational / Parkland
	Cemetery

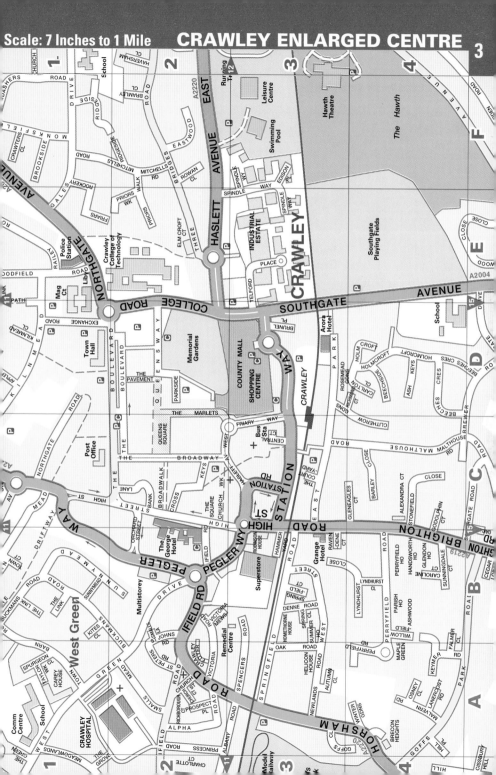

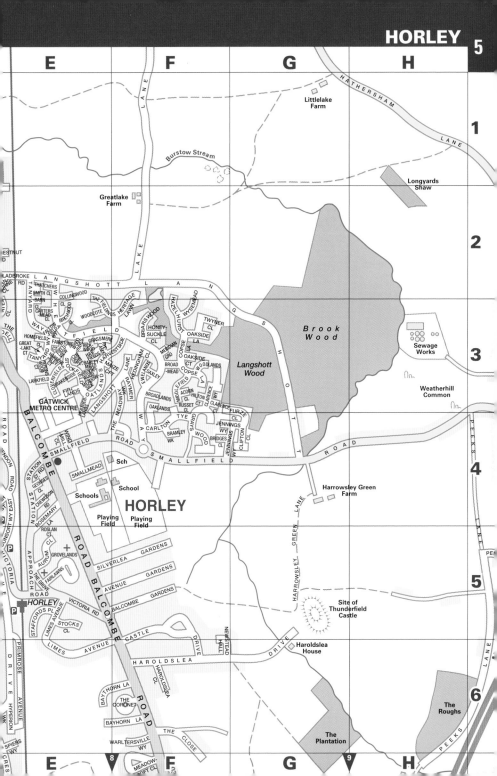

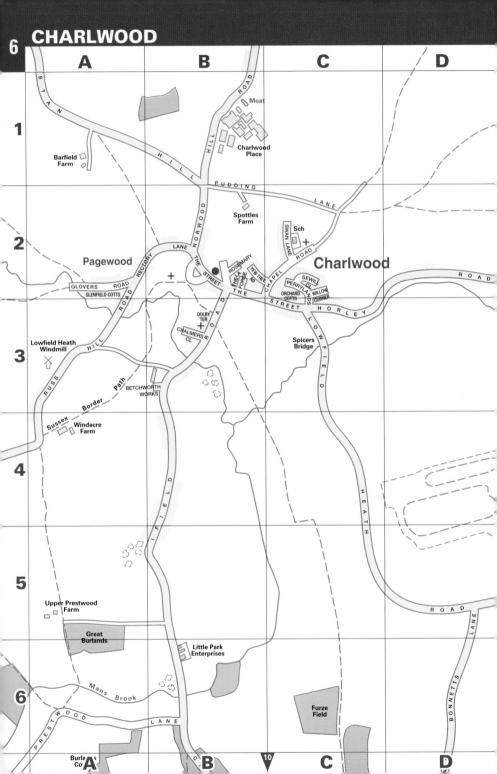

A B C D

1

STAN

Barfield
Farm

HILL ROAD

HILL

NORWOOD

Moat

Charlwood
Place

PUDDING LANE

Spottles
Farm

2

Pagewood

RECTORY LANE

THE STREET

ROSEMARY

THE
FORGE RD

YEW TREE

SWAN LANE

Sch

Charlwood

CHAPEL ROAD

SEWILL CL
PERRYLANDS
ORCHARD WILLOW
COTTS CORNER

GLOVERS ROAD

GLENFIELD COTTS

THE STREET

HORLEY ROAD

ROAD

3

Lowfield Heath
Windmill

RUSS HILL ROAD

Border Path

Sussex

Windacre
Farm

DOLBY
TER

CHALMERS
CL

THE ROAD

BETCHWORTH
WORKS

Spicers
Bridge

LOWFIELD

HEATH

4

IFIELD

5

Upper Prestwood
Farm

ROAD

LANE

Great
Burlands

Little Park
Enterprises

BONNETTS LANE

6

Mans Brook

PRESTWOOD LANE

Furze
Field

Burla...
Co...

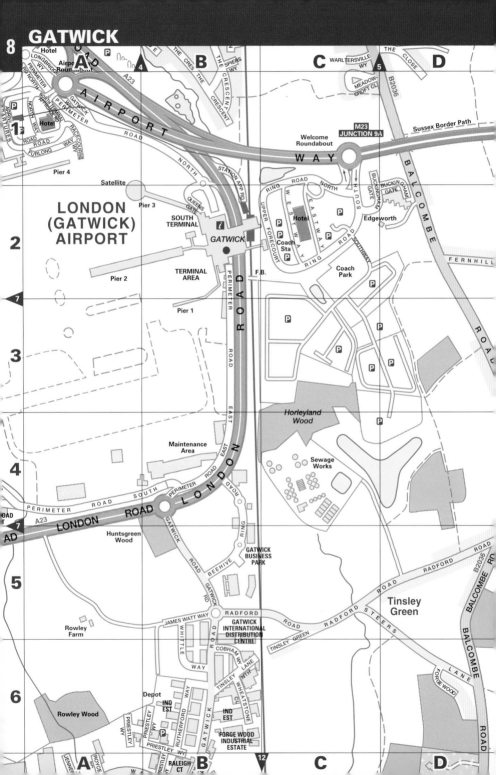

The Plantation

Peeks Rough Farm

E **5** **F** **G** **H**

M23

M23 JUNCTION 9

Bellhatch Wood

BROADBRIDGE

1

Bridges Wood

DOWNLANDS

CHURCH

ROAD

DONKEY LANE

Burstow

LANE

Moat

Moat

CHURCH

LANE

2

Fernhill

PEEKS

ROAD

Sch

PEEKS

CHURCH

GREEN

LANE

CHURCH

LANE

B2037

ROAD

LANE

3

M23

Burstow Hall

LANE

Shipley Bridge

ANTLANDS
LA WEST

Kiln Heath

Newhouse Farm

ANTLANDS ROAD

ANTLANDS LANE EAST

ANTLANDS

LANE

B2037

BALCOMBE ROAD

Shipley Bridge

BRIDGE

Golf Course

Burstow Farm

4

Playing Field

5

SHIPLEY

Wellfield Copse

Rec Grnd

BANK

BORERS

22

ST FRA

NS RD

SHIPLEY BRIDGE LANE

ELGER WY

ROFFEYS CL

CHART WOOD

COPTHORNE

CHURCH RD

Sch

THE GLEBE

BEECHEY WAY

6

OAK CLOSE

DAWN RISE

THE MEADOW

MEADOW

CHURCH

LANE

THE GREEN

THE LINDENS

BEECHEY CL

PINE TREES

WESTWAY

BROOKSIDE

BROOKHILL

THE MEADOW

NEW TOWN NEW

KNOWLE

Co

BRIDGELANDS

BROOK VIEW

AKEHURST CL

CHURCH LA

Sch

Co

Heathy Ground

ERICA WAY

ERICA

DRIVE

BROOKHILL CL

BRACKEN LANE

FAIRWAY

COPTHORNE

TOWN

THE GABLES

E **F** **13** **G** **H** **COP**

A   B   C   D

1
Burlands Copse
Ifield Wood
Cophall Wood
Ifield Hall
The Brook
Club
Crawley R.F.C

2
Ifieldwood
Ifield Court Farm
Moat
Ifield Court Hotel
Strafford Bridge
RIVER MEAD
STRATHMORE RD
Pockneys Farm

3
River Mole
Ifield Green
Cricket Ground
MILL LA
RECTORY LA
TWEED LA
OLD MANOR CL
Sch
LANGLEY
KIRKFORD
HARDHAM
FRAMFIELD

Bonwycks Place

4
The Grove
Ifield Brook
RUSPERS KEEP
PARHAM
PATCHING ROAD
LOXWOOD
LAVINGTON CL
STORR INGTON
LINCHMERE
LANCING
WARREN
FRISTON
ALBERT CR CT
DEERSWOOD CT
DRIVE
LADY MARGARET RD
NUTHURST CL
MID HURST
Scho
School
Ifield

RUSPER
Furlong Farm

5
Ifield Golf Course
Playing Field
BUDG WICK RD
SHIPLEY ROAD
SELHAM CL
SLINFOLD WK
SOUTHWATER CL
SHIPLEY WK
Sch
Playing Field
IFIELD
Golf and Country Club
WHITEHALL DR
MERLIN
LANCELOT
EXCALIBUR RD
GUINEVERE
SHARPTHORNE CL
TANGMERE RD
TREYFORD CL
OVERDENE DRIVE

6
de Hill
Hyde Hill Brook
RUSPER ROAD
Ifield Mill
STAN BRIDGE
GALAHAD
MIDDLETON CL
BEAUMONT
ST ANDREWS RD
BIRKDALE CL
HOY-LAKE CL
PREST WICK CL
DOBBINS
PUFFIN
BUTTERMERE
RYDE
DEWAR CL
STRODLAND
Ifield Mill
Nursing Home
THE MILLBANK
THE MILLBANK
HILLMEAD
PARKFIELD
HIGHAMS HILL
THE CROFT
PRIEST CROFT
NURSERYLANDS
HAZELWOOD
GOSSOPS GRN LA
FILBERT CRESCENT
COB WK
PICK-FIELD
RICK-FIELD DRIVE
LOVE
OATLANDS
MEADOWCROFT
THE
HOLLOW
HAMS HILL
WINDY RIDGE
CHERWELL
RUTHER
CUCKMERE CRESCENT
GOSSOPS
DAIRY FIELDS
POLLARDS
RYELANDS
DOWER WK
OATLANDS
DERWENT CL
KENNET
MEDWAY RD
CRESCENT
PADDOCKHURST ROAD
HASCOMBE CT
DUNSFOLD
Comm Centre
LEA CL
MEDWA
CUCKMERE
CAPEL LANE
KID
Sch
Playir Field
HANS
Moor Park Cres

CRAWLE

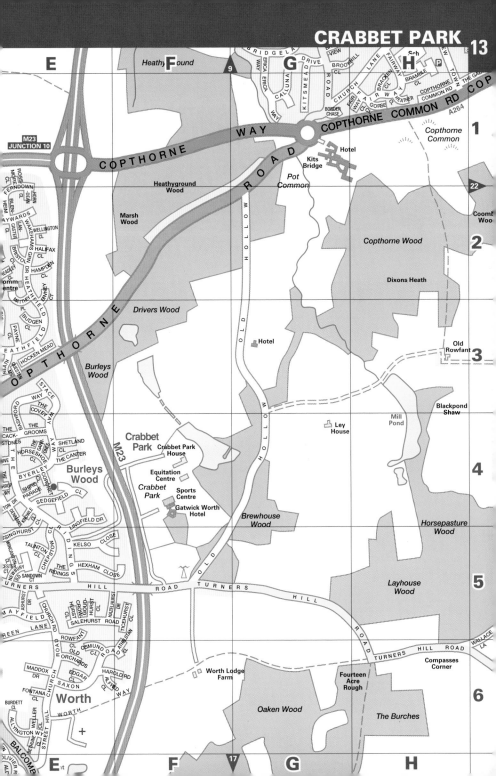

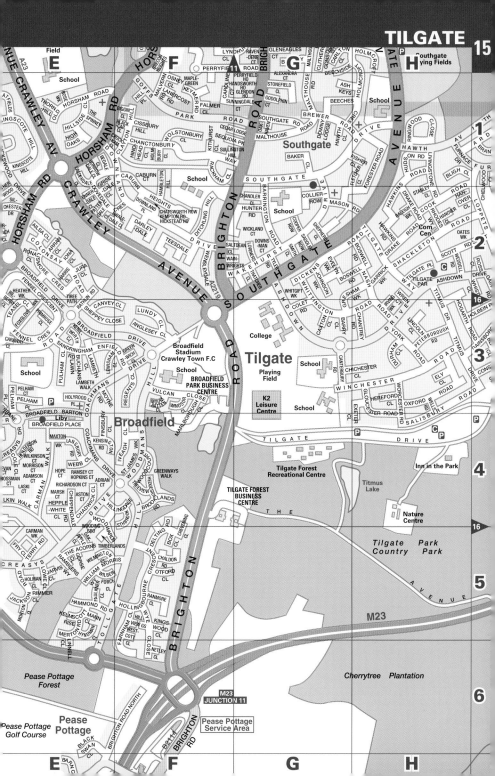

Field

E **F** **A** **G** **H**

School

LYNDU
RAVEN-
DENE
GLENEAGLES
PERRYFIELD
PERRYFIELD
RD
LANERCOST
MALVERN
OSNEY
MAPLE-
GREEN
KEYMER RD
CAROLINE
HANDSWORTH
HO
CLUTHER
GUNSTOO
CARLTON
ALEXANDRA
CT
STONEFIELD
GODOLPHIN
MALTHOUSE
CT
BEECHSIDE
HOLMCROFT
ASH
KEYS
BEECHES
School

Horsham Road

THORN
HILL
HORSHAM ROAD
HILLSIDE
THE SPINNEY
HIGH OAKS

BIGGIN
HILL
GOFFS
PARK
HILL
LANERCOST
RD
FALMER
ROAD
SOUTHGATE
RD
CEDAR LODGE
BREWER
DOWN
LODGE
RINGWOOD
CLOSE
HAWTH
LIVINGSTONE
RD
STANLEY
FURNACE
DR
BLIGH CL
BRAN

CRAWLEY AV

CROWBOROUGH
HILL
BLACK
OAKS
CISSBURY
HILL
WOLSTONBURY
KITHURST
SEQUOIA PK
SOUTHGATE
MALTHOUSE
FISHER
HAWTH
ON RD
HANOVER
ROAD

HORSHAM RD

AILSA CL
COLONSAY
ARRAN
IONA
JURA
CHANCTONBURY
HINDHEAD
HOLM
BURY
RACKHAM
School
CHANDLER
HUNTER
RD
COLLIER-
ROW
MASON
DR
HAWKINS
FORESTER ROAD
FLETCHER
HAWTH
DRAKE ROAD
COOK
RHODES
OATES
WK
SCOTT
WEDDELL
ROSS CL
WHISTLER

CRAWLEY

RONALD CL
COLONSAY
HARRIS
IONA
RATHLIN
TREE PATH
BROADFIELD DRIVE
HEIGHTS
CABURN
DOWNLAND
DALE
GRISE
PATTERDALE
DALE
CRES
SWALE
DARLEY
DALE
TEESDALE
CHATSWORTH ROW
KEMPTON HO
HICKSTEAD HO
DITCHLING DRIVE
WENSLEYDALE
WAKE
SOUTHGATE
BARRINGTON RD
WICKLAND
CT
DOWNS-
MAN
WAIN-
WRIGHTS
SALTDEAN
LORIMERS
COPPER
ROW
SADDLER
ROW
SMITH
DICKENS WK
JOHNSON
WK
HAWKINS
BOSWELL
NASH
BOSWELL
TILGATE ROAD
GARRICK
WK
SHACKLETON
TILGATE
PAR
ASHDOWN
DRIVE

FENNEL CRESCENT
HEATHER
CL
BERKELEY
CL
TEASEL
CL
FOXGLOVE
PRIMROSE
CARAWAY
FENNEL
CRES
CANVEY CL
SHEPPEY CLOSE
LUNDY CL
ANGLESEY CL
GREEN
WICH
EVELYN
WK
WHITGIFT
WK
COLET
WK
WHITTINGTON
GRESHAM WK
IRVING
WREN
YORK ROAD
LINCOLN
PETERBOROUGH
RD
TITMUS
HOGARTH ROAD
GAINSBOROUGH
HOLBEIN

BROADFIELD
SANDRINGHAM
ENFIELD
LEWISHAM
School
College
BARRY
CHANTREY
CANTERBURY
ROAD
CHICHESTER
CL
HEREFORD
ROAD
OXFORD
WELBY
ELY
CL
SALISBURY
CONS

School
Broadfield
Stadium
Crawley Town F.C
School
BROADFIELD
PARK BUSINESS
CENTRE
Tilgate
Playing
Field
School
WINCHESTER
GLOUCESTER
EXETER
WORCESTER RD

PELHAM
PL
CARMANS
HOLYROOD
VULCAN
MARLBOROUGH
CLOSE
MOUNT
PL
WINDSOR DRIVE
Broadfield
School
K2
Leisure
Centre
School

FULHAM
BUCHANS
ROLAND
LAMBETH
ROAD
LAMBETH
WALK
REGENTS
FINSBURY
BARTON
Liby
BROADFIELD
PLACE
TILGATE
DRIVE

MAXTON
WK
LAMSBURY
WEBB
COACHMANS
DRIVE
IVEAGH
WK
GREENWAYS
WALK
Tilgate Forest
Recreational Centre
Inn in the Park

CREASYS
KILFERSON
WILKINSON
CT
MORRISON
CT
ADAMSON
CT
LASKI
CT
EVANS
HOPE
RAMSEY CT
HOPKINS CT
ADRIAN
CL
ST JAMES WK
WOODMANS
MERRYWEATHER
HESSELGREAVE
WK
Titmus
Lake

LKIN WALK
CARMAN
MARSH
HEPPLE-
WHITE
CL
RICHARDSON CT
CHIPPENDALE
ASTON
CL
CHADWICK
WOODWARDS
HILLINGDALE
BROOKLANDS
TILGATE FOREST
BUSINESS
CENTRE
Nature
Centre

CARMAN
WK
FRY CL
CLERRY RD
THE ACORNS
APPLETREE
TIMBERLANDS
WOODBINE CL
DELTING
BOX
CL
CHERRING
THE
Tilgate Park
Country Park

CREASYS
LOWE CL
RAMBLERS
JARVIS WK
WILMINGTON
WILLIAM
WILBER
FORCE
MORRIS
INGS
CRES
CHALDON
CL
OTFORD
CL
RANMORE
AVENUE
16

CARMAN
FRY CL
RIMMER
CL
JACKSON
CL
MONTON CL
HOLMAN
HAMMOND RD
HOLLINGBOURNE
WILBER
FORCE
HILL
KINGS
WOOD
M23

KELMSCOT
MANN
MERTON RD
RISE
LINNELL
FARNHAM
CL
WELL
MEW
GS
NETLEY
CL
Cherrytree Plantation

BRIGHTON ROAD

Pease Pottage
Forest

BRIGHTON
RD

M23
JUNCTION 11

Pease Pottage
Golf Course
Pease
Pottage
BLACK
SWAN
BRIGHTON ROAD NORTH
A2114
BRIGHTON
RD
Pease Pottage
Service Area
BARNC

E **F** **G** **H**

Southgate

Tilgate

HORSHAM RD

BRIGHTON ROAD

SOUTHGATE

CRAWLEY AVENUE

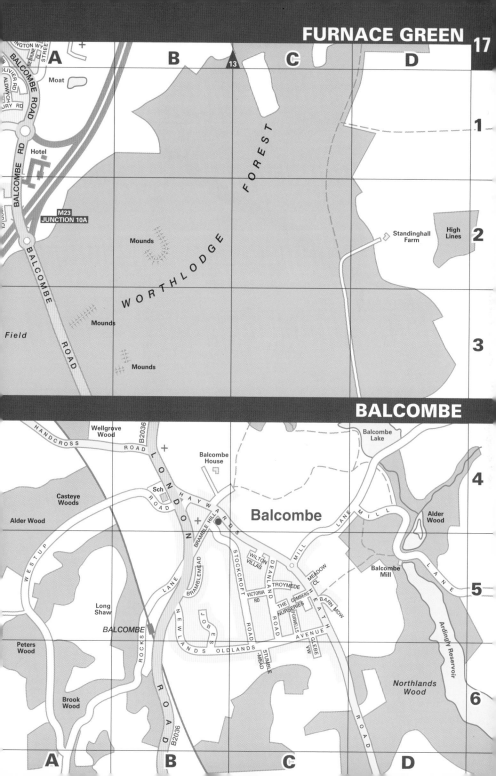

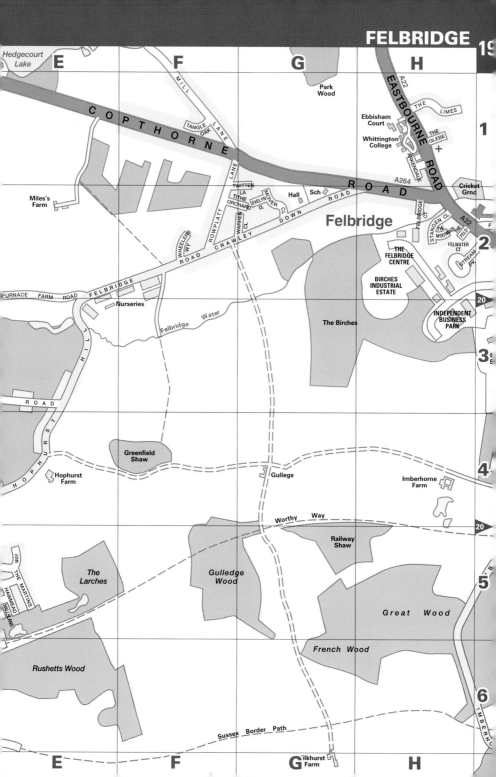

Hedgecourt Lake

E **F** **G** **H**

MILL LANE

Park Wood

A22

THE LIMES

C O P T H O R N E

TANGLE OAK LANE

Ebbisham Court

EASTBOURNE ROAD

THE GLEBE

1

Whittington College

ARKENDALE

Miles's Farm

R O A D

A264

TWITTEN

LA TITHE ORCHARD

MOVER CL

Hall

Sch

ROAD

Felbridge

STANDEN CL

THE MOORINGS

THE FIELD

Cricket Grnd

F

EVELYNN CL

WHEELERS WY

ROWPLATT

LANE

WARREN CL

CRAWLEY

DOWN

FELBRIDGE CT

FELWATER CT

STREAM PK

A22

2

FELBRIDGE ROAD

THE FELBRIDGE CENTRE

FURNACE FARM ROAD

ROAD

Nurseries

BIRCHES INDUSTRIAL ESTATE

20

HOPHURST HILL

Felbridge Water

The Birches

INDEPENDENT BUSINESS PARK

3

t S

ROAD

Greenfield Shaw

4

Hophurst Farm

Gullege

Imberhorne Farm

20

Worthy Way

Railway Shaw

WAY

THE MARTINS

HAWMEAD

HALSLAND

The Larches

Gulledge Wood

Great Wood

5

B

Rushetts Wood

French Wood

6

IMBERH

Sussex Border Path

Gilkhurst Farm

E **F** **G** **H**

E **F** **G** **H**

Swites Wood

Blackhatch Wood

HILL

1

BORDER CT
THE WEALD
SPRING WY
WOODLANDS ROAD
SANDHAWES
THE LARCHES
HOLLANDS WY
HOSKIN
HOLTYE AVENUE
QUARRY RISE
PACKER
CSE
DART CT

Stonequarry

Orchards Farm

A264

ROAD HOLTYE **ROAD**

BEECHFIELDS

HOLTYE

LANCASTER
BLENHEIM
FULMAR
HOLTYE PL
STIRLING WY

QUEEN VICTORIA HOSPITAL

ST MARGARET'S
ELIZABETH FARM

GREENSTEDE AV
CRESCENT

MERIDAN WY

TURNER CT
MERLIN WY
PEGASUS WY
HILLARY DRIVE
PEGASUS
DRIVE
KINDERSLEY

2

LANCASTER AVENUE

HOLLOW
ROAD

LYNTON RISE
CL
PARK GLEAVE

LYNTON
LYNTON AVENUE

Cemy

HOLTYE

Ashplats Wood

Fairlight Farm

Blackwell RD

Pol Sta

Amb Sta
Council Offices
Meridian Hall

Football Grnd

Fairlight Wood

3

CRANSTON RD

STONE-LEIGH CL

Playing Fields

MINDLEHEIM AV
SAN FELIU
WOODBURY AV
VERBANIA WY

COLLEGE LANE

COLLEGE LANE
WESTCOTS
GIFFARDS CL
CRES
COURT CL
LUCAS
WABG CRES
DENE

DRIVE
CHESTNUT CL
MAPLE DR
HARMANS
WATERSIDE

Theatre

DE LA WARR RD
CHEQUER RD
P
ST SWITHUNS CL
P
Coll
LAUREL
WARLTON
OLD RD
ELM DR
BOURG-DE-PEAGE
SYCAMORE DR
HARMANS MEAD
COURT YARD
THE DRIVE

AVENUE

4

LEWES
RD
CHURCHLANE
+
LEWES
STREET
SACKVILLE CT
FAIRFIELD RD
LEWES RD

Sch
Sackville School

WARBURTON
LOWER DENE
AVENUE
BENCHFIELD CL
BROOK CL
WOODBURY DRIVE
THE O
FARM CL
FARM
THE GLADES

Pitlands Wood

ROAD

LANE

DE
MARTYNS PL
TANYARD AV
OAKS CL
OAKCROFT
WOODBURY CL

LEWES

Worsted Farm

Fowl Wood

5

KINGSBERRY
RISER
HERON
RICHMOND
CORNWALL
GLOUCESTER CL
KINGS COPSE
AVENUE
SANDRINGHAM CT
HERON CL
WAY
BARTON CRES

LOWER MERE
MALLARD PL
NORMANDY CL
WILLOW MEAD
YORK
WINDSOR
HOLLYWOOD

GLENDYNE
DRIVE
GLENDYNE

WORSTED LA
OAKLEY CL

HERONTYE

STUART CL
CROMWELL
REGAL DR
TUDOR CL
HAMPTON WY
CAVALIER

DRIVE

BUCKINGHAM DR
BALMORAL

Brockenhurst

Nursing Home

LANE

Berry Wood

22

6

HARWOODS LA
PRINCE
GEORGE
VICTORIA
EDINBURGH
COLLINGWOOD

Herontye

Sussex Border Path

A22

HECTORS LANE

WELLFIELD

WINDMILL LA

Beeches Farm

CHESTERTON
HARWOODS LA

WEALDEN HOUSE

LANE

THE ROCKS
DENE LANE
BEECHES

E **F** **G** 22 **H**

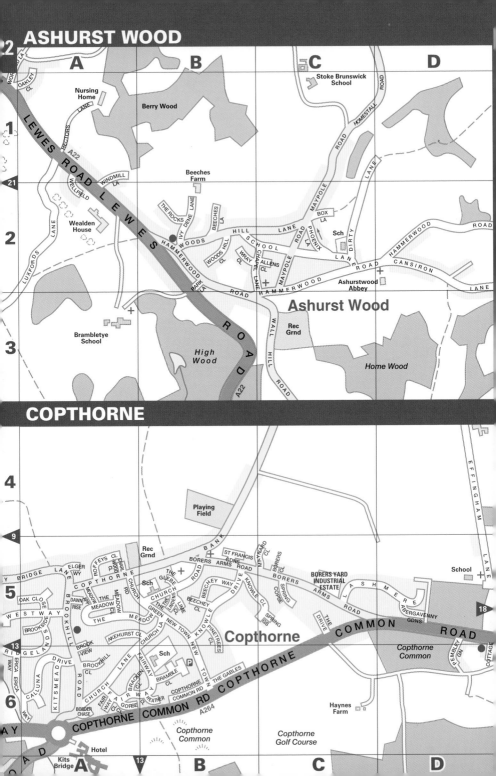

22

A   B   C   D

Stoke Brunswick School

Nursing Home

Berry Wood

1

LEWES ROAD

OAKLEY CL

HECTORS LANE

A22

WINDMILL LA

WELLFIELD

21

LUXFORDS

LANE

Wealden House

THE ROCKS

IVY DENE LANE

Beeches Farm

BEECHES LA

HILL

SCHOOL

LANE

CHAPEL LA

WRAY CL

ALLENS CL

MAYPOLE ROAD

PHOENIX LA

BOX LA

Sch

DIRTY LANE

HAMMERWOOD

ROAD

CANSIRON LANE

2

LEWES

HAMMERWOOD

WOODS

WOODS CL

MAYPOLE

HAMMERWOOD ROAD

Ashurstwood Abbey

Bramletye School

PARK LA

ROAD

A22

High Wood

Ashurst Wood

WALL HILL ROAD

Rec Grnd

Home Wood

3

A   B   C   D

4

Playing Field

EFFINGHAM LANE

9

Rec Grnd

BRIDGE LANE

ELGER WY

ROFFEYS CL

COPTHORNE

WOOD CL

CHURCH RD

THE GLEBE

Sch

BANK ROAD

ST FRANCIS GDNS

BORERS ARMS ROAD

MY MEAD

BORERS CL

BORERS

BORERS ARMS ROAD

BORERS YARD INDUSTRIAL ESTATE

LASHMERE ROAD

School

18

5

OAK CLOSE

WESTWAY

DAWN RISE

MEADOW

THE MEADOW

THE MEADOW

BEECHEY WAY

BEECHEY CL

THE LINDENS

CHURCH LA

NEW TOWN

NEW

KNOWLE CL

SPRING COPSE

SPRING GS

THE DRIVE

COMMON ROAD

ABERGAVENNY GDNS

Copthorne Common

PEMBLEY GN

COTTAGE

BROOKSIDE

BROOKHILL

AKEHURST CL

Copthorne

13

RIDGELANDS

ERICA WAY

CALUNA

ERICA

KITSMEAD

DRIVE

BROOK VIEW

BROOKHILL CL

CHURCH ROAD

FAIRWAY

FAIR WAY

BRACKEN LA

Sch

P

BRAMBLE CL

HEATHER

GORSE

COPTHORNE COMMON RD

THE GABLES

NEW TOWN

COPTHORNE COMMON RD

COPTHORNE COMMON ROAD

Haynes Farm

Copthorne Common

Copthorne Golf Course

6

BOIDER CHASE

WAY

ROAD

Kits Bridge

Hotel

A264

13

A   B   C   D

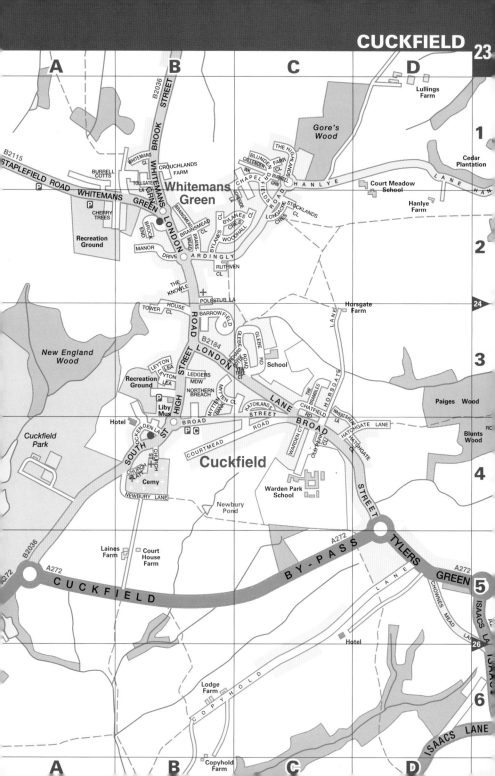

Lullings Farm

Gore's Wood

Cedar Plantation

1

B2036 BROOK STREET

B2115

STAPLEFIELD ROAD

WHITEMANS GREEN

WHITEMANS GRN

BURRELL COTTS

CHERRY TREES

Recreation Ground

Whitemans Green

CROUCHLANDS FARM

TOULGATE LA

WHITEMANS CL

LONDON

BROCK END

MANOR DRIVE

ARDINGLY

BRAINSMEAD

BRAINS CL

BYLANES CL

WOODHALL

CHAPEL FIELDS ROAD

BLUNDEN FARR

CALLENDER SQ

THE HIGHLANDS

BURRELL GRN

HANLYE

Court Meadow School

Hanlye Farm

STOCKLANDS CL

LONGACRE CRES

2

RUTHVEN CL

THE KNOWLE

TOWER CL

HOUSE CL

POLESTUB LA

BARROW FIELD

B2184

LONDON ROAD

HIGH STREET

New England Wood

Horsgate Farm

24

LEYTON LEA

LEYTON LEA

Recreation Ground

LEDGERS MDW

NORTHERN BREACH

MYTTEN CL

MYTTEN LA

GLEBE RD

GLEBE ROAD

YEW TREE CT

School

Paiges Wood

3

Liby Mus

Hotel

BROAD ST

OCKENDEN LA

Cuckfield Park

SOUTH ST

CHURCH ST

CHURCH PLATT

Cemy

NEWBURY LANE

COURTMEAD

HATCHLANDS STREET

BROAD ROAD

WARDEN CT

CHATFIELD RD

THE BRAMBLES

HORSGATE LANE

WHEATSHEAF

OLD PARK CL

HATCHGATE CL

HATCHGATE

Blunts Wood

RC

4

Cuckfield

Newbury Pond

Warden Park School

B2036

A272

A272

CUCKFIELD

Laines Farm

Court House Farm

BY - PASS

A272

BY - PASS

STREET

TYLERS GREEN

A272

CHOWNES MEAD

ISAACS LA

5

Hotel

26

ISAACS LANE

Lodge Farm

COPYHOLD

6

Copyhold Farm

ISAACS LANE

A   B   C   D

1

Borde Hill Gardens

COPYHOLD LANE

Copyhold Bridge

Wickham Wood

Sugworth Farm

Sugworth Wood

Staves Copse

Haywards Heath Golf Course

SANDRIDGE LA

BEECH

Flat Wood

Bitchen Wood

THE DRIVE

Club Ho

ROUNDWOOD LANE

2

Lullings Gorse

Spring Copse

BORDE HILL LANE

BALCOMBE

BROOK LANE

HIGH

PORTSMOUTH WOOD

BARRINGTON WD

SUNTE

Cedar Plantation

HANLYE

GATESMEAD

BY

23

Penland Farm

ORCHARD WAY

FAIRFIELD

OAKHURST LA

WAY

ORCHARD CL

BIRCHEN LANE

SUNTE

OAK BANK

3

THE SPINNEY

PENLAND

THE CEDARS

SUGWORTH RD

BARNMEAD ROAD

OLD WICKHAM LA

BALCOMBE ROAD

MILL HILL

WICKHAM

CLOSE

GANDER GRN

HILL

SUMMERHILL LA

Tavistock & Summerhill School

SUMMERHILL GRANGE

SUMMERHILL CL

B2028

Sports Ground

Harlands School

Penland Wood

PENLAND AVON

PENLAND TURNERS CL

BARNMEAD

BRIDGERS

MILL

HILL CL

WICKHAM MILL

COLLEGE ROAD

GANDER

SUMMERHILL

BRIDGE ROAD

COMMON

4

QUARRY HILL

HARLANDS CL

PENLAND

Haywards Heath College

The Ashdown

BURRELL

BRIDGE ROAD BUSINESS PARK

GORDON ROAD

Amb Sta

QUEENS CT

WEST

GREENWAY

23

WOOD

HARLANDS ROAD

LUCASTES

PASTURE HILL ROAD

BANNISTER WY

TURNERS

BURRELL ROAD

Supermarket

MILL GREEN

Fire Sta

MILL GREEN ROAD

QUEENS

CHURCH

ROAD

OTTAFIELD CT

Blunts Wood

BLUNTS WOOD CRES

THE DROVEWAY

GREAT HEATHMEAD

MARKET PLACE

COMMERCIAL SQ

SYDNEY RD

PK

OATHALL

ST PAULS AVENUE

5

ROSEMARY CL

HILLSIDE WK

LUCASTES LANE

WOOD

THE DELL

LUCAS GRANGE

CULROSS AV

WINNALLS PK

MILTON RD

MARKET RD

HAYWARDS HEATH

CLEVELANDS

ST CLAIR RD

CLAIR CT

Cricket Ground

Comm. Centre & Theatre

FARLINGTON

ST PAULS AV

FARLINGTON

AVENUE

LINCOLN

HEATHERBANK

SERGISON RD

ROAD

AVENUE

1.BYRON CT
2.CHAUCER CT
3.KIPLING CT
4.SHELLEY CT
5.TENNYSON CT
6.MILTON CT

BODIAM CT

The Heath Recreation Ground

St Pauls R.C. School

LITTLE

WOOD

FOXWARREN DR

BADGER DR

SHERWOOD DR

CHILLIS WOOD

LUCASTES WY

WYCHPERRY RD

OAKLANDS RD

HUSTON RD

NEWTON RD

JIREH

HEATH

ARBOR

FAIRFORD

Haywards Heath

HIGH TREES

BENTSWOOD ROAD

6

TYLERS GRN

ISAACS LA

A273

A272

BUTLERS GREEN RD

Playing Fields

Pol Sta & Mag Court

Beech Hurst Recreation Ground

MUSTER GREEN STH

WEALDEN

THE BOWER

THE LAURELS

Nursing Home

NURSERY CL

PADDOCKHALL RD

Liby

Council Offices

T.H.

NORTH

THE BROADWAY

PERRYMOUNT ROAD

SOUTH ROAD SOUTH

CHELSEA ARC

HIGHAND

CHURCH ROAD

Health Centre

ST JOSEPHS

ST WILFRIDS WAY

QUEENS WAY

OAKWOOD

SPRINGFIELD RD

HAZELGROVE WAY

CLOVER LEA

HAZEL GROVE GDNS

MAYFLOWER WAY

FIELDS END

WOODLANDS

Hayworth School

HOLLYWOOD

TREVELYAN RD

GLADEPOINT

Victoria Park Recreation Ground

AUGUSTINE WAY

PINEHAM COPSE

BLUEBELL

PRIORY

IND EST

Sch

26

E F G H

Sargie Wood
Kenwards Farm
Bridge Wood
Grange Farm
Court Wood
Paxhill Park
BUXHALLS HILL
PARK LANE
STREET
B2028

1

Kiln Wood
Town Wood
Lindfield Bridge
Nunnery Wood
SPRING LA
Weir
Mill

FINCHES GDS
SPRING
WELKIN
Old Place
FINCHES GDS
FINCHES PARK
GREEN MDWS
THE WELKIN
THE WELKIN
WELKIN
SPRING LANE
Lindfield
Hangman's Acre

2

BARRINGTON
SAVILL
FINCHES
GAVILL RD
Playing Fields
HICKMAN RD
MAIN
SHENSTONE
FRANCIS
THE WILDERNESS
DUKES
BRUSHES LA

SUNTE
BROOKWAY
PICKERS
PICKERS GRN
GLEBE
DENMANS
HICKMANS LA
COMPTON RD
TOLLGATE
Mus
ALMA RD
DUKES BARN CT
CHALONER
NEWTON
NEWTON
Little Walstead Farm

3

CHESTNUT
APPLEDORE
The CHESTNUTS
SUMMERHILL DR
OAKFIELD
AVENUE
HICKMANS LA
Mus
C
Liby
OLD SCHOOL CT
CHALONER
HARVEST
LUXFORD RD
LIME TREE GROVE
EASTERN RD
EASTERN RD
EASTERN LANE
ROAD

WEST COMMON
BLACK HILL
COMMON
PELHAM PL
LITTLE BLACK HILL
PONDCROFT
HIGH
LEWES
Schools
Lindfield Common
WEST VIEW RD
NOAHS ARK
ARK LA
East VIEW
East WICK
Little Walstead Farm

4

FRENCH GDNS
BLACKTHORNS
APPLEDORE
BLACKTHORNS CL
School
BECKWORTH
BECKWORTH CL
BACKWOODS CL
LINDEN GRO
BACKWOODS LANE
MEADOW LANE
GREY DRIVE
ALDERSEY RD
West VIEW COTTS
SCAMPS
LINDFIELD ENTERPRISE PARK
Walstead Grange
Walstead Common
Cemy
MASCALLS
SNOWFLAKES LA
ROAD

Oathall Community College
PELHAM GARDENS
CROXTON LANE
MEADOW LANE
ALLEN LANE
Walstead
EAST LEWES

Playing Fields
PENN
CRES
WILMINGTON WY
HAVLAND RD
WILLIAM LANE
LAWRIE
CRIPLAND CL
COOMBERS
RIG'T LINGS
ORCHARD
HILL ROAD

5

ASHINGTON
BENTSWOOD
BENTSWOOD CRES
ROAD
HANBURY
AMERICA
BARN COTTAGE
CRES
Playing Field
AMERICA LANE
WESTLANDS RD
GRAVELYE LANE
THE PLATT
Walstead Manor

AMERI
PILGRIM
CL
BOSTON
AMERICA LANE
HOLLOW LANE
KILN LA
THE RISE
KNOLL
PLG'R
ALYOTH
LANE
BEDALES HILL
B2111

ALLEN
BOSTON CT
Hunbury Park Sports Centre
SILVER BIRCHS
THE COPSE
WILLOW LANE
NORTHLANDS
BEECH
THE PINES
Bedales
ROAD

6

AMERI CL
RIDGE
JUB'LEE CL
ROAD
SILVER
POND WALK
REED
ASHDOWN
CEDAR LA
OAKS LA
THE MARLOW
SNOWDROP LANE
A272
Cud Fa

Cemetery
Franklands Village
Hall
GRAVELYE LANE
NORTHLANDS AV
HOBLAND
LARCH WY
CATKIN
DRIVE
CHAR
Lyoth Common

E F **27** G H AD

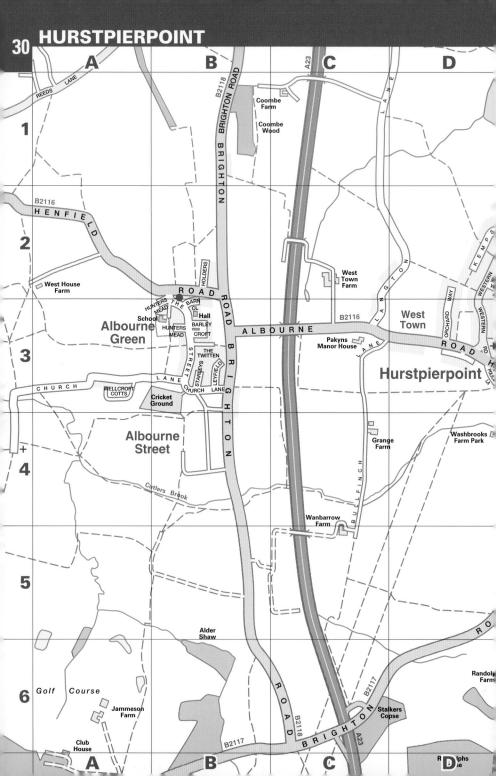

A B C D

REEDS LANE

B2118

BRIGHTON ROAD

A23

1

Coombe Farm

Coombe Wood

B2116

H E N F I E L D

BRIGHTON

2

KEMPS

West House Farm

West Town Farm

LANGTON

WESTERN

HOLDERS

ROAD

WESTERN

ORCHARD WAY

RD

R O A D

THE BARN

HUNTERS MEAD

Albourne Green

School

HUNTERS MEAD

CL

BARLEY CROFT

Hall

ALBOURNE

B2116

West Town

3

STREET

THE TWITTEN

STAPLEYS

LEYFIELD

BRIGHTON

Pakyns Manor House

LANE

R O A D

Hurstpierpoint

LA

CHURCH

LANE

CHURCH

LANE

WELLCROFT COTTS

Cricket Ground

4

Albourne Street

Cutlers Brook

R O A D

Grange Farm

Washbrooks Farm Park

BULFINCH

Wanbarrow Farm

5

6

Golf Course

Alder Shaw

R O A D

B2117

Randolphs Farm

Jammeson Farm

Club House

B2117

BRIGHTON ROAD

A23

B2118

Stalkers Copse

Rndolphs se

A B C D

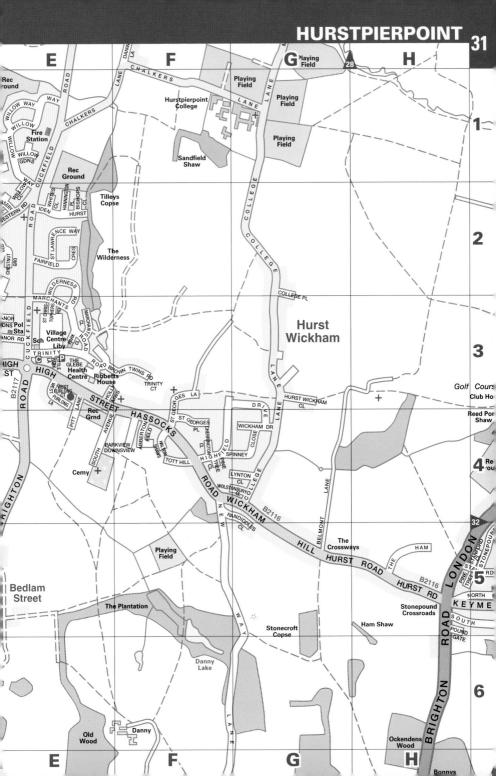

A   **B**   **C**   **D**

Golf Course
Club House

Reed Pond
Shaw

Rec
Ground

Hassocks

Keymer

HAM

HURST RD

B2116

Stonepound
Crossroads

LONDON ROAD

BRIGHTON ROAD

KEYMER

NORTH
BANK

SOUTH
POUND
GATE

m Shaw

Ockendens
Wood

Bonnys
Wood

Lag Wood

Butchers
Wood

Clayton

B2112

NEW

CLAYTON HILL

UNDER HILL

SPRING LA

Clayton
Windmills

Clayton Holt

SHEPHERDS WALK

THE BOURNE

BANKSIDE

THE SPINNEY

THE MEADOWS

THE BRAMBLES

THE CROFT

SHEPHERDS

LITTLE PRIORY

FRIARS

ABBOTS

OAK RD

COPSE

FRIARS

RD

GRACE CT

BELMONT CT

PAVILION CL

STANFORD

PINE TREES

STONEPOUND

STANFORD

NORTH
COURT

FARM

RAVENSWOOD

SEMLEY

SAMPSONS

STATION COTTS

WOODSLAND

CLAYTON PK

STATION APP

WEST

BTA APP

STATION APP EAST

KINGS

QUEENS DR

CHANCELLORS

WOODSLAND ROAD

PARK

HASSOCKS ROAD

Sch

GRAND DRIVE

THE CLOSE

ORCHARD LANE

WILMINGTON CL

ADASTRA

Adastra
Grounds

AVENUE

FARNHAM AV

ANN CL

MANOR

BROMLEY CL

MACKIE

OCKLEY

SWEET-
LANDS

OCKLEY WY

OLDLANDS AV

THE QUADRANT

FIR TREE

FIR TREE WY

PARKSIDE

CLERKS ACRE

KEYMER GDNS

CLERKS ACRE

THE ACRE

Keymer

WAY

DAMIAN MEAD

NEWLANDS CL

Playing
Field

Liby

Coll

CHURCH ROAD

THE CRES

SILVERDALE

KEYMER PK

BEACON
-HURST

CLAYTON

THE ORCHARD

OCKENDEN

LAGWOOD CL

BONNY RD

WOOD

WAY

DOWNS

VIEW ROAD

PARKLANDS

WINDMILL

BROOK AV

DALE AV

ORION PAR

THE MINNELS

WILLOW

BROOK WY

HIGHLANDS CL

THE PILLARS

STAFFORD WY

ST ANNS GDNS

LODGE LANE

School

School

Playing field

Fire
Station

PARK AV

LODGE ROAD

LANE

Lodge Farm

Millbrook
Shaw

MILL

E   F   G   H

1

2

3

4

5

6

Court Gardens Farm

B2112

LANE

SOUTHVIEW

COMMON

END

NORTH

ORCHARD LA

B2112

DUMBRELLS CT RD

DUMBRELLS CT

LODGE HILL

Lodge Hill

Sussex Border Path

Stocks Farm

SPATHAM LANE

Nurseries

Ditchling

BODDINGTON LA

EAST GDNS

THE DYMOCKS

EAST

Mus

CHURCH LA

LANE

Pol Sta

MULBERRY LA

THE TWITTEN

HIGH ST

S ST

WEST ST

SOUTH ST

LEWES

ROAD

BRANGWYNS

END

BRANGWYN ACRE

FIELDWAY

FARM LA

Stoneywish Country Park

East End

B2116

EYMER

ROAD

THE DROVE

Cricket Ground

Hall

CHARLTON GDNS

School

BARNFIELD GDNS

LANE

East End Playing Field

Cemy

SPATHAM

ROAD

LEWES

B2116

B2112

LAYTON

ROAD

NEVILL COTTS

CHR

LONG PK

BEACON

ROAD

INYE

LANE

SHIRLEYS

Blackdog Hill

Molehilly Shaw

Jointer Copse

The Nye

Nurseries

Wellcroft Shaw

Westmeston Place

Park Barn Farm

BEACON

LANE

UNDERHILL

NYE LA

UPPER BEACON

ROAD

Wick Farm

UNDERHILL

Burnthouse Borstall

LANE

B2116

ROAD

LEWES

THE STREET

Westmeston

E   F   G   H

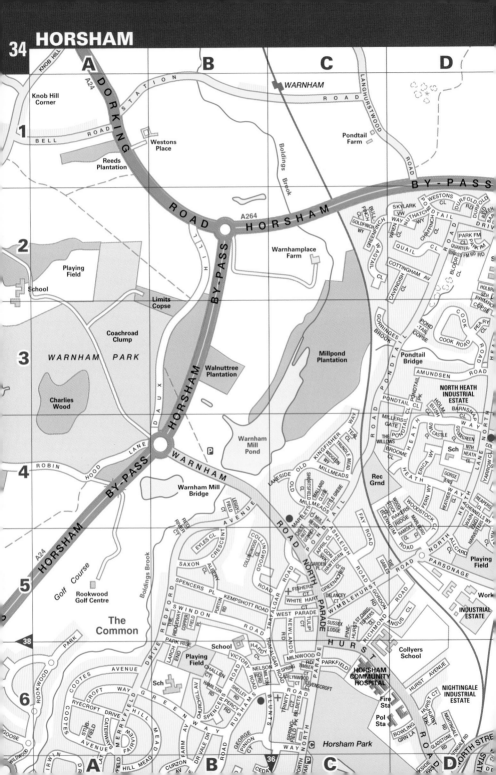

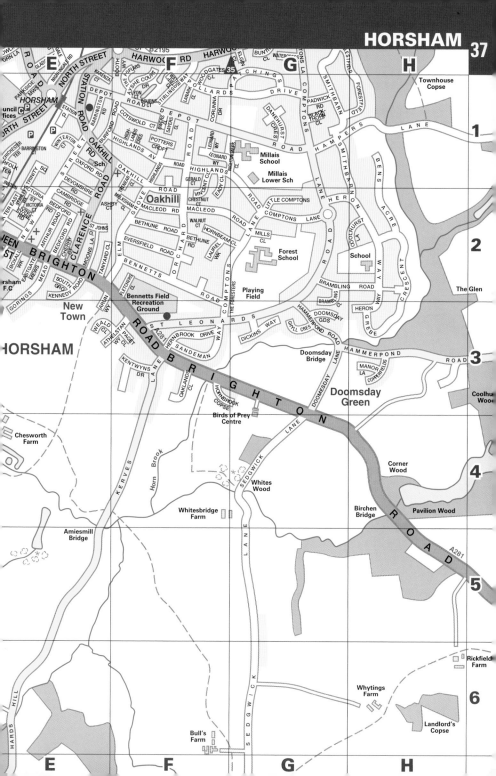

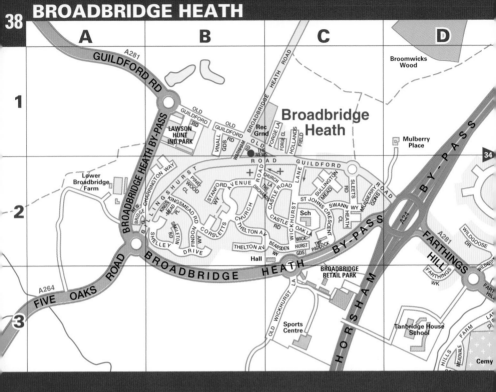

INDEX TO STREETS
with Postcodes

The Index includes some names for which there is insufficient space on the maps. These names are indicated by an * and are followed by the nearest adjoining thoroughfare.

Abberton Fld BN6 31 F4
Abbots CI BN6 32 B1
Abbotsbury Ct RH13 35 E6
Abbotsfield Rd RH11 14 A1
Abergavenny Gdns
  RH10 22 D5
Abinger Keep*,
  Langshott La RH6 5 E3
Abrahams Rd RH11 14 D5
Acorn CI,
  East Grinstead RH19 20 D5
Acorn CI, Horley RH6 5 F3
Acorns RH13 35 G5
Acre CI RH16 26 B3
Adamson Ct RH11 15 E4
Adastra Av BN6 32 C2
Adelaide CI,
  Crawley RH11 11 G2
Adelaide CI,
  Horsham RH12 35 F5
Adelphi CI RH10 16 D1
Admiral Rd RH11 14 D2
Adrian Ct RH11 15 E4
Adur Rd RH15 29 F3
Agate La RH12 35 E4
Ailsa CI RH11 15 E2
Aintree Rd RH10 16 A1
Airport Way RH6 8 A1
Akehurst CI RH10 22 A5
Albany Rd RH11 3 A2
Albert CI RH16 27 E1
Albert Crane Ct RH11 10 D4
Albert Dr RH15 28 B5

Albert Rd RH6 4 D3
Albery CI RH12 34 B5
Albion CI RH10 12 D6
Albion Ct RH15 28 D4
Albion Way RH12 36 C1
Albourne Rd BN6 30 C3

Alder CI RH10 18 D6
Alder Copse RH12 36 A3
Alders Av RH19 20 C2
Alders View Dr RH19 20 D2
Aldingbourne CI RH11 10 C4
Aldwych CI RH10 17 E1
Alexandra Ct RH11 3 C4
Alexandra Rd RH15 29 F4
Alfred CI RH12 13 E6
Alicia Av RH10 12 C5
Allcard CI RH12 34 D5
Allcot CI RH11 14 B2
Allen Rd RH16 25 E6
Allens CI RH19 22 C2
Allingham Gdns RH12 35 G4
Allyington Way RH10 13 E6
Alma Rd RH16 25 F3
Almond CI RH11 10 D6
Alpha Rd RH11 3 A2
Amberley CI,
  Burgess Hill RH15 28 D2
Amberley CI,
  Crawley RH10 12 D5
Amberley CI,
  Haywards Heath RH16 26 B1
Amberley CI,
  Horsham RH12 35 G3
Amberley Rd RH12 35 G3
Ambleside CI RH11 14 A1
America La RH16 25 E6
Amundsen Rd RH12 34 D3
Anchor CI RH12 36 D2
Andromeda CI RH11 14 B2
Angell CI RH10 12 C6

Anglesey CI RH11 15 F3
Angus CI RH12 34 C5
Ann CI BN6 32 D1
Antlands La RH6 9 E3
Antlands La East RH6 9 F4
Antlands La West RH6 9 E3
Appledore Ct RH16 25 E3
Appledore Gdns RH16 25 E4
Applefield RH10 3 D1
April CI RH12 34 C5
Aquarius Ct RH11 14 B2
Arbor Ct RH16 24 C6
Archers Ct RH10 11 G3
Arcturus Rd RH11 14 B2
Arden Rd RH10 16 A1
Ardingly CI RH11 11 E3
Ardingly Rd RH17 23 B2
Argus Walk RH11 14 D2
Arkendale RH19 19 H1
Arne CI RH11 14 C2
Arne Gro RH6 4 B2
Arnfield CI RH11 10 B6
Arnside RH12 36 B2
Arrals CI RH10 18 D5
Arran CI RH11 15 E2
Arran Ct RH12 36 C1
Arrivals Rd RH6 7 H1
Artel Cft RH10 12 A5
Arthur Rd, Crawley RH11 10 B5
Arthur Rd,
  Horsham RH13 37 E2
Arun Way RH13 37 E3
Arundel CI RH10 12 C5
Arundel Ct RH11 28 C3
Arundel Mews RH16 26 D2
Arunside RH12 36 B2
Ash CI RH10 18 D5
Ash Gro RH16 26 B2
Ash Keys RH10 3 D4
Ash Rd RH16 12 B3
Ash Way RH15 28 D5
Ashburnham Rd RH10 16 B1
Ashby Dr RH13 37 E2
Ashdown CI RH16 25 F6

Ashdown Ct RH10 16 A2
Ashdown Dr RH10 15 G2
Ashdown Vw RH19 20 D6
Ashenground CI RH16 26 C2
Ashenground Rd RH16 26 B2
Ashleigh CI RH6 4 C4
Ashleigh Rd RH12 34 C5
Ashurst CI RH12 35 G4
Ashurst Dr RH10 13 E5
Ashurst PI RH16 24 C6
Ashwood RH11 3 B4
Aspen CI RH15 27 F1
Aspen Walk RH16 27 F1
Aspen Way RH12 35 E5
Aspley Ct*,
  Ellman Rd RH11 14 C2
Assisi Ct RH16 26 D2
Aston Ct RH11 15 E4
Athelstan CI RH10 13 F6
Athelstan Way RH13 37 E3
Atkinson Rd RH10 16 C1
Auckland CI RH11 11 G3
Augustines Way RH16 26 D1
Aurum CI RH6 5 E5
Austen CI RH19 20 A4
Autumn CI RH11 3 A3
Avebury CI RH12 35 G2
Aveling CI RH10 16 C1
Avenue Gdns RH6 5 E5
Aviary Way RH10 18 D5
Avon Walk RH11 10 C6
Avondale CI RH16 4 C2
Avonhurst RH15 29 F4
Ayshe Court Dr RH13 37 F1

Backwoods CI RH16 25 F4
Backwoods La RH16 25 F4
Baden Dr RH6 4 B3
Badger Dr RH16 24 A5
Badgers CI RH12 35 E3
Badgers Walk RH15 29 G5
Badgers Way RH19 20 D2

Bailey CI RH12 35 F2
Baird CI RH10 12 B2
Bakehouse Barn CI
  RH12 34 D2
Bakehouse Rd RH6 4 C2
Baker CI RH10 15 G1
Balcombe Ct RH10 12 D5
Balcombe Gdns RH6 5 F5
Balcombe Rd,
  Crawley RH6,10 8 D1
Balcombe Rd,
  Haywards Heath RH16 24 B2
Balcombe Rd,
  Horley RH6 5 E4
Baldwin CI RH10 16 D2
Baldwins Fld RH19 20 B1
Balliol CI RH10 12 D2
Balmoral RH19 21 F5
Bancroft Rd RH10 12 D6
Bank La RH11 3 C2
Banks Rd RH10 12 C6
Bankside BN6 32 B1
Bannister Way RH16 24 C4
Barber CI RH10 16 C3
Barkdale RH15 29 G2
Barley Cft BN6 30 B3
Barley CI RH10 3 C4
Barley Dr RH15 28 A3
Barley Mead RH6 5 E3
Barlow Rd RH11 14 B2
Barn CI BN6 30 B3
Barn Cottage La RH16 25 E6
Barnard Gate RH16 24 C4
Barnes Mews RH12 36 C*
Barnfield Gdns RH16 33 G3
Barnfield Rd RH10 11 G4
Barnmead RH16 24 B3
Barnside Av RH15 29 G6
Barnsnap CI RH12 34 D3
Barnwood RH10 12 C6
Barons Ct RH15 29 E4

Name	Ref	Name	Ref	Name	Ref	Name	Ref	Name	Ref
Barrackfield Walk RH12	36 C3	Billinton Dr,		Border Ct RH19	21 E1	Broadbridge La RH6	9 H1	By Sunte RH16	24 D2
Barrington CI RH16	25 E2	Crawley RH10	12 C6	Borers Arms Rd RH10	22 B5	**Broadbridge**		Bycroft Way RH10	12 B4
Barrington Ct RH12	37 E1	Billinton Dr,		Borers CI RH10	22 C5	**Retail Pk RH12**	**38 C3**	Byerley Way RH10	13 E4
Barrington Rd,		Crawley RH10	16 C1	**Borers Yard Ind Est**		Broadfield Barton RH11	15 E4	Bylanes CI RH17	23 B2
Crawley RH10	15 G1	Binney Ct RH10	13 E3	**RH10**	**22 C5**	Broadfield Dr RH11	15 E2	Bylanes Cres RH17	23 B2
Barrington Rd,		Binstead CI RH11	11 E3	Borrowdale CI RH11	15 E1	Broadfield PI RH11	15 F3	Byrd Rd RH11	14 C2
Haywards Heath RH16	25 E2	Birch Av RH17	27 E2	Bosham Rd RH10	16 D2	**Broadfield Pk**		Byron CI, Crawley RH10	12 C4
Barrington Rd,		Birch CI, Crawley RH10	18 D6	Bostock Av RH12	35 G5	**Bsns Centre RH11**	**15 F3**	Byron CI,	
Horsham RH13	37 E1	Birch CI,		Boston CI RH16	25 E6	Broadlands RH6	5 F3	Horsham RH12	35 E3
Barrington Wood RH16	24 D2	Haywards Heath RH17	27 F1	Boston Rd RH16	25 E6	Broadmead RH6	5 F3	Byron Ct RH16	24 C5
Barrowfield RH17	27 F1	Birch Lea RH10	12 B2	Boswell CI RH12	15 G2	Broadwalk RH10	3 C2	Byron Gro RH19	20 B4
Barry CI RH10	15 G3	Birch Way RH17	27 E2	Bough Beeches RH15	29 F6	Broadwood CI RH12	35 H4		
Bartholomew Way RH12	35 F3	Birchen La RH16	24 D3	Boundary Rd RH10	11 H4	Broadwood Rise RH11	14 D4	**C**	
Barton Cres RH19	21 F5	Birches Rd RH12	35 H4	Bourg-de-Peage Av		Brock End RH17	23 B2	Caburn Ct RH11	15 F1
Barton Walk*,		**Birches Ind Est RH19**	**19 H2**	RH19	21 E4	Brock Rd RH11	11 E3	Caburn Heights RH11	15 F1
Norwich Rd RH10	16 B1	Birchwood CI,		Bourns Ct RH13	37 F1	Brockham Keep*,		Caffins CI RH11	11 H4
Bartlelot Ct RH12	36 D2	Crawley RH10	16 D3	Bowater Rd RH10	16 D3	Langshott La RH6	5 E3	Calbourne RH16	24 B6
Bartlelot Rd RH12	36 D2	Birchwood CI,		Bowers PI RH10	18 C5	Brockhurst CI RH12	36 A2	Caldbeck Ho RH11	14 C3
Bashford Way RH10	13 E4	Horley RH6	5 E3	Bowes CI RH13	35 E6	Bromley CI BN6	32 C2	Calderdale CI RH11	15 E1
Basildon Way RH11	14 B3	Birchwood Grove Rd		Bowling Green La RH12	35 G4	Brook Av BN6	32 C3	Caledonian Ho*,	
Bassett Rd RH10	16 D2	RH15	29 F6	Bowman CI RH10	11 G4	Brook La RH14	24 D2	London Rd RH11	11 G3
Bateman Ct RH10	16 B2	Birdham CI RH11	11 E3	Bowness CI RH11	14 A1	Brook Rd RH12	35 E3	Callender Wk RH17	23 C1
Baxter CI RH10	16 C1	Birkdale Dr RH11	10 A6	Box CI RH11	15 F5	Brook St RH17	23 B1	Callisto CI RH11	14 B2
Bay CI RH6	4 B1	Bisham CI RH10	16 D2	Box La RH19	22 C2	Brookhill CI RH10	22 A6	Calluna Dr RH10	22 A6
Bay Tree Ct RH10	16 D1	Bishopric RH12	36 C1	Boxall Walk RH13	37 E2	Brookhill Rd RH10	22 A5	Caltswood La RH16	26 A2
Bayfield Rd RH6	4 B3	Bishopric Ct RH12	36 C1	Bracken CI,		Brooklands Rd RH11	15 F4	Calvin Walk RH11	14 B2
Bayhorn La RH6	5 E6	Bishops CI BN6	31 E2	Copthorne RH10	22 A6	Brooklands Way RH10	20 C5	Camber CI RH10	12 D5
Baylis Cres RH15	28 B2	Bishops Ct RH12	36 C2	Bracken CI,		Brookside,		Cambridge Rd RH13	37 E2
Bayhorn La RH6	5 E6	Bitmead CI RH11	10 B6	Crawley RH10	11 H3	Copthorne RH10	22 A5	Camelot Ct RH11	10 C5
Beachy Rd RH11	14 D4	Bittern CI RH11	10 A6	Bracken Gro RH12	35 H4	Brookside, Crawley RH10	3 F1	Campbell Cres RH19	20 A4
Beacon Ct RH12	35 G5	Black Dog Walk RH10	11 G3	Bracknell Walk RH11	14 B3	Brookside,		Campbell Rd RH10	16 C1
Beacon Rd BN6	33 F3	Black Hill RH16	25 E3	Bradbury Rd RH10	16 C3	Crawley Down RH10	18 D6	Campion Rd RH12	34 D4
Beaconhurst BN6	32 D3	Black Swan CI RH11	15 E6	Brainsmead RH17	23 B2	Brookview RH10	22 D4	Canberra CI RH11	11 G3
Beale CI RH11	14 D2	Blackbird CI RH15	28 A4	Brainsmead RH17	23 B2	Brookview RH10	22 D4	Canberra PI RH12	35 F5
Beale St RH15	28 C5	Blackbridge La RH12	36 C2	Brakenside RH6	5 E3	Brookway,		Cansiron La RH19	22 D2
Bearsden Way RH12	38 C2	Blackbridge La RH12	36 B2	Bramber CI,		Burgess Hill RH15	29 F3	Cantelupe Mews*,	
Beaumont CI RH11	10 B6	Blackcap CI RH11	15 F1	Crawley RH10	11 H3	Brookway,		Cantelupe Rd RH19	20 D4
Beaver CI RH12	35 E3	Blackett Rd RH10	12 C6	Bramber CI,		Haywards Heath RH16	25 E4	Cantelupe Rd RH19	20 D4
Beckett La RH11	11 F2	Blackfold Rd RH10	12 A6	Haywards Heath RH16	24 B6	Brookwood RH6	5 E3	Canterbury Rd RH10	15 G3
Beckett Way*,		Blackheath RH10	12 D3	Bramber CI,		Broomdashers Rd RH10	3 F1	Cants CI RH15	29 G3
Stuart Way RH19	21 E5	Blackhorse Way RH12	36 C1	Horsham RH12	35 G4	Broome Ct RH10	34 C4	Cants La RH15	29 F3
Beckford Way RH10	16 C4	Blackhouse La RH15	29 E3	Bramber Way RH15	28 D2	Brown Twins Rd RH10	31 E3	Canvey CI RH11	15 E3
Beckworth CI RH16	25 E4	Blackstone Way RH15	28 D2	Bramble Gdns RH15	28 B3	Browning CI RH10	12 C4	Capel La RH11	14 C1
Beckworth La RH16	25 E4	Blackthorn CI,		Bramble Hill RH17	17 B5	Browns Wood RH19	20 D1	Capenors RH15	28 C6
Bedale CI RH11	15 E1	Crawley RH11	11 F3	Bramblemead RH17	17 B5	Bruce CI RH16	26 C2	Capricorn CI RH11	14 B2
Bedales Hill RH16	25 H6	Blackthorn CI,		Brambles BN6	32 B1	Brunel Centre RH10	12 A2	Capsey Rd RH11	10 B6
Bedelands RH15	29 F2	Horsham RH13	37 G1	Brambletye Rd RH10	12 A6	Brunel PI RH10	3 D3	Caraway CI RH11	15 E3
Bedford Rd RH13	37 E2	Blackthorns,		Brambling CI RH13	37 G3	Brunswick CI RH10	16 A1	Carey Ho RH11	3 A1
Beech Gdns RH10	18 C6	Hassocks BN6	31 E1	Brambling Rd RH13	37 G2	Brunswick Ct*,		Carfax RH12	36 D2
Beech Hill RH16	25 F6	Blackthorns,		Bramley CI RH10	3 F2	Brunswick CI RH10	16 A1	Cargo Forecourt Rd RH6	7 F2
Beech Holme RH10	18 C6	Haywards Heath RH16	25 E4	Bramley Walk RH6	5 F4	Brushes La RH16	25 F3	Cargo Rd RH6	7 G2
Beech Hurst CI RH16	24 B6	Blackthorns,		Brandon CI RH10	16 D1	Brushwood Rd RH12	35 H3	Carlton CI RH10	3 D4
Beech Rd RH12	35 H4	Haywards Heath RH16	25 E4	Brnagwyns Acre BN6	33 G3	Bryce CI RH12	35 H3	Carlton Ct RH6	4 D2
Beech Tree CI RH10	11 G4	Blackwall Farm Rd RH19	20 D2	Brantridge Rd RH10	16 A1	Buchans Lawn RH11	15 E3	Carlton Tye RH6	5 F4
Beeches Cres RH10	3 D4	Blackwell Hollow RH19	21 E3	Bray CI RH10	16 D2	Buckhurst CI RH19	20 B2	Carman Walk RH11	15 E4
Beeches La RH19	22 B2	Blackwater La RH10	12 D5			Buckhurst Mead RH19	20 B1	Caroline CI RH11	3 B4
Beechey Rd RH10	16 A3	Blake CI RH10	16 A3	**Braybon**		Buckhurst Way RH19	20 B2	Carter Rd RH10	16 D2
Beechey Way RH10	22 B5	Blatchford CI RH13	35 E6	**Bsns Pk RH15**	**28 C5**	Buckingham Dr RH19	20 C5	Cartersmead CI RH6	5 E3
Beechfields RH19	21 E1	Blatchford Rd RH13	35 E6	Brecon Heights RH11	3 A4	Buckingham Gate RH6	8 C1	Casher Rd RH10	16 C2
Beeching Way RH19	20 C4	Blenheim CI,		Breezehurst Dr RH11	14 B2	Buckley PI RH10	18 C5	Castle Dr RH6	5 F6
Beechside RH10	3 D4	Crawley RH10	13 E2	Bremner Av RH15	4 C3	Buckmans Rd RH11	3 A2	Castle Rd RH12	38 C2
Beechwoods RH15	29 E6	Blenheim CI,		Brettingham Ct RH11	14 B2	Buckswood Dr RH11	14 C1	Caterways RH12	34 A6
Beeding CI RH10	35 G4	East Grinstead RH19	21 F2	Bretton RH15	28 B2	Budgen CI RH10	13 E3	Catkin Way RH16	27 F1
Beehive Ring Rd RH6	8 B5	Blenheim Mews RH10	26 D2	Brewer Rd RH10	15 G1	Bulbeck CI RH15	28 C5	Cavalier Way RH19	21 E5
Behenna CI RH11	14 B1	Blenheim Rd RH12	34 C4	Breydon Walk*,		Bullfinch CI, Horley RH6	4 B3	Cavell Way RH10	16 C1
Bell Centre RH10	12 A1	Bligh CI RH10	15 H1	Norwich Rd RH10	16 B1	Bullfinch CI,		Cavendish CI RH12	34 D2
Bell Hammer RH19	20 D4	Blindley Rd RH10	12 D3	Briar CI RH11	11 F3	Horsham RH12	34 C2	Cavendish Ho RH16	26 D2
Bell Rd RH12	34 A1	Bloor CI RH10	34 D2	Briars Wood RH6	5 F3	Bullfinch La BN6	30 C4	Caxton CI RH10	15 G3
Bellamy Rd RH10	16 C3	Blount Av RH19	20 B4	Briarswood CI RH10	12 D4	Bunbury CI RH19	35 F6	Caxton Way RH16	26 D1
Belloc Ct RH12	12 C4	Bluebell CI,		Brickfield La RH6	4 A6	Bunyan CI RH11	14 B2		
Belloc Ct RH13	35 G6	Crawley RH10	14 D3	Bricklands RH10	18 C6	Burbeach CI RH11	15 E2	Cedar CI,	
Belmont CI BN6	32 B1	Bluebell CI,		Brickyard La RH10	18 C6	Burchetts CI RH16	26 C3	Burgess Hill RH15	29 F2
Belmont La BN6	31 G5	East Grinstead RH19	20 A4	Brideake CI RH11	14 D3	Burdett CI RH10	13 E6	Cedar CI, Crawley RH11	11 F2
Belvedere Ct RH10	12 B5	Bluebell CI,		Bridge CI RH15	28 D2	Burdock CI RH11	14 D3	Cedar CI,	
Belvedere Walk RH6	26 A1	Haywards Heath RH16	24 D6	Bridge Rd RH16	24 D4	Burdocks Dr RH15	29 G5	Horsham RH12	36 C1
Benchfield CI RH19	21 F4	Bluett Rd RH10	16 A3	**Bridge Rd**		Burford Rd RH13	37 E1	Cedar Lodge RH11	15 F1
Benhams CI RH6	4 D2	Blundell Av RH6	4 C3	**Bsns Pk RH16**	**24 C4**	Burgh Ct RH10	13 E2	Cedar Way RH16	25 F6
Benhams Dr RH6	4 D2	Bluebell Way RH11	28 A2	Bridgelands RH10	9 G6	Burlands RH11	10 D2	Celandine CI RH11	14 D3
Benjamin Rd RH10	16 D1	Blundell CI RH11	4 C3	Bridgers Mill RH16	24 B4	Burleigh CI RH10	18 D5	Central CI RH10	3 C3
Bennett CI RH10	16 C3	Blunden Dr RH17	23 C1	Bridges CI RH6	5 F4	Burleigh Way RH10	18 C6	Chadwick CI RH11	15 E4
Bennetts Rd RH13	37 F2	Blunts Way RH12	34 B6	Bridges CI RH12	35 F4	Burleys Rd RH10	12 D5	Chaffinch CI,	
Bens Acre RH13	37 H1	Blunts Wood Cres RH16	24 A4	Bridle Way RH10	12 D4	Burma CI RH16	27 G1	Burgess Hill RH15	28 B2
Bentswood Cres RH16	25 E5	Blunts Wood Rd RH16	24 A5	Brighton Rd,		Burners CI RH15	29 G5	Chaffinch CI,	
Bentswood Rd RH16	24 D6	Boddington La BN6	33 F3	Crawley RH10	3 B4	Burney Ct*,		Crawley RH11	11 F3
Berkeley CI RH11	14 B3	Bodiam CI RH10	12 D5	Brighton Rd,		Kingsley Rd RH11	14 D2	Chaffinch CI,	
Berry CI RH12	29 E2	Bodiam Ct RH16	24 C5	Hassocks BN6	32 A4	Burns CI RH12	35 E3	Horsham RH12	34 D2
Berrymeade Walk*,		Bolding Way RH16	26 C3	Brighton Rd,		Burns Rd RH10	12 C3	Chaffinch Way RH6	4 B3
Drummond Rd RH11	10 B6	Boleyn CI RH10	16 D2	Horley RH6	4 C5	Burns Way RH19	20 B4	Chailey CI RH11	14 D3
Berstead Walk RH11	14 C2	Bolney CI RH11	14 C2	Brighton Rd,		Burrell Cotts RH17	23 A1	Chaldon Rd RH11	15 F5
Betchley CI RH19	20 C2	Bolnore Rd RH16	26 A1	Horsham RH13	37 E2	Burrell CI RH11	14 C2	Chalkers La RH16	31 E1
Betchworth Works RH6	6 A3	Bolnore Rd RH16	26 A1	Brighton Rd,		Burrell Grn RH17	23 C1	Challen CI RH12	34 B6
Bethune CI RH16	13 E6	Bolnore Village RH16	26 A1	Hurstpierpoint BN6	30 B1	Burrell Rd RH16	24 B4	Challow CI BN6	32 A2
Bethune Rd RH13	37 F2	Bolters Rd RH6	4 C2	Brighton Rd North RH16	15 E6	Burston Gdns RH19	20 C1	Chalmers CI RH6	6 B3
Betts Way RH10	11 G1	Bolters Rd South RH6	4 C2	Brisbane CI RH11	11 G2	Burstow Ho*,		Chaloner CI RH16	25 F3
Bevan CI RH11	15 E4	Bolton Rd RH10	16 C4	Bristol CI RH10	13 E2	Skipton Way RH6	5 E2	Chaloner Rd RH16	25 F3
Beverley Mews RH10	12 A6	Boltro Rd RH16	24 B6	Britten CI, Crawley RH10	14 C2	Burton CI RH6	4 D5	Chancellors Pk BN6	32 B2
Bewbush CI RH11	14 B2	Bonehurst Rd RH6	4 D1	Britten CI,		Burwash Rd RH10	12 A6	Chanctonbury Rd RH15	29 F6
Bewbush PI RH11	14 C2	Bonnetts La RH11	6 D6	Horsham RH13	35 H5	Bush La RH12	35 F1	Chanctonbury Way	
Bickley Ct RH11	14 D3	Bonny Wood Rd BN6	32 B3	Broad Green Av RH15	29 F5	Butlers Green Rd RH16	24 A6	RH11	15 F1
Biggin CI RH11	15 F1	Booth Rd RH11	14 B2	Broad St RH17	23 B4	Butlers Rd RH13	35 G5	Chandler CI RH11	15 G2
Bignor CI RH12	35 G3	Booth Way RH13	37 F1	Broadbridge Heath By-Pass		Butterfield RH19	20 A2	Chantlers CI RH19	20 B3
Bilberry CI RH11	15 E2	Borage CI RH11	14 D3	RH13	38 A2	Buttermere CI RH13	35 G3	Chantrey Rd RH10	15 H3
Bilbets RH12	34 C6	Borde Hill La RH16	24 B2	Broadbridge Heath Rd		Butts CI RH11	11 E5	Chantry CI RH6	4 C3
Billingshurst Rd RH12	38 A2	Border Chase RH10	22 A6	RH12	38 B1	Buxshalls Hill RH16	25 G1	Chapel CI RH15	28 D2
								Chapel La,	
								Crawley RH10	18 A2

39

Chapel La,
East Grinstead RH19 22 C2
Chapel Rd RH6 6 C2
Chapelfields RH17 23 C1
Chapman Rd RH10 16 C3
Chapmans La,
East Grinstead RH19 20 A3
Chapmans La,
East Grinstead RH19 20 C3
Charles Av RH15 28 B4
Charlesfield Rd RH6 4 C3
Charleston St RH10 16 B2
Charlesworth Pk RH16 27 G1
Charlock Cl RH11 14 D3
Charlotte Ct*,
Leopold Rd RH11 11 F5
Charlton Gdns BN6 33 F3
Charlwood Cl RH10 22 A5
Charlwood Gdns RH15 29 F1
Charlwood Rd,
Burgess Hill RH15 29 G1
Charlwood Rd,
Horley RH6 7 F1
Charlwood Rd,
Ifield RH11 10 B1
Charlwood Rd,
Lowfield Heath RH11 7 E5
Charlwood Walk RH11 11 D1
Charlwoods
Bsns Pk RH19 20 C2
Charlwoods Pl RH19 20 C2
Charlwoods Rd RH19 20 C2
Charm Cl RH6 4 B3
Charmans Cl RH12 38 G5
Charrington Way RH12 38 B2
Chatelet Cl RH6 5 E3
Chatfield Rd RH17 23 C3
Chatfields RH11 15 E1
Chatsworth Row RH11 15 F2
Chaucer Av RH19 20 B4
Chaucer Cl RH16 24 C5
Chaucer Rd RH10 12 C3
Chelsea Arc RH16 24 C6
Chelwood Cl RH10 16 A2
Chennells Way RH12 34 D4
Chepstow Cl RH10 13 E5
Chequer Rd RH19 21 E4
Chequers Cl RH6 4 D3
Chequers Dr RH6 4 D3
Cherrington Cl BN6 31 F4
Cherry Cl RH15 28 B4
Cherry Ct RH13 37 E2
Cherry La RH11 11 F2
Cherry Tree Walk RH12 35 G3
Cherrytree Cl RH10 12 D4
Cherwell Walk RH11 10 C6
Chesterfield Cl RH19 18 D1
Chesters RH6 4 B2
Chesterton Ct RH19 21 E6
Chestnut Cl,
Burgess Hill RH15 29 F2
Chestnut Cl,
East Grinstead RH19 21 F3
Chestnut Ct RH13 37 F2
Chestnut Gdns RH12 34 C5
Chestnut Gro BN6 31 E2
Chestnut Rd RH6 5 E2
Chestnut Walk RH11 11 F2
Chestnuts Cl RH16 25 E3
Chesworth Cl RH13 36 D3
Chesworth Cres RH13 36 D3
Chesworth Gdns RH13 36 D3
Chesworth La RH13 36 D2
Chetwood Rd RH11 14 B3
Chevening Cl RH11 11 E5
Cheviot Walk RH11 11 E5
Cheyne Walk RH6 4 C6
Cheynell Walk RH11 14 C1
Chichester Cl RH16 15 G3
Chichester Ter RH12 37 E1
Chichester Way RH15 29 G1
Chiddingly Cl RH10 12 B6
Chilcomb RH15 29 F6
Chillis Wood Rd RH16 24 A5
Chiltern Cl RH11 11 E5
Chiltington Cl RH15 28 D2
Chippendale Rd RH11 15 E4
Chownes Mead La
RH16 23 D5
Christies RH19 20 B4
Christopher Rd RH19 20 D4
Church Av RH16 24 C4
Church Cl RH15 28 D4
Church Ct, Crawley RH11 3 A2
Church Ct,
Haywards Heath RH16 24 C6
Church La,
Albourne BN6 30 A3
Church La,
Copthorne RH10 22 A6
Church La,
Crawley RH10 12 A5

Church La,
Ditchling BN6 33 F3
Church La,
East Grinstead RH19 21 E4
Church La,
Haywards Heath RH17 26 D6
Church La, Horley RH6 9 E2
Church La,
Horsham RH12 38 B2
Church Mead BN6 32 D3
Church Platt RH17 23 B4
Church Rd,
Broadbridge Heath
RH12 38 B2
Church Rd,
Burgess Hill RH15 29 E4
Church Rd, Burstow RH6 9 G1
Church Rd,
Crawley RH10 22 A5
Church Rd,
Haywards Heath RH16 24 C6
Church Rd, Horley RH6 4 C5
Church Rd,
Horsham RH12 35 H4
Church Rd,
Lowfield Heath RH6 7 H4
Church Rd
Ind Est RH11 7 H4
Church Rd
Trading Est RH11 7 H4
Church St, Crawley RH11 3 A2
Church St,
Haywards Heath RH17 23 B4
Church Walk,
Burgess Hill RH15 28 D4
Church Walk,
Crawley RH10 3 C2
Church Walk, Horley RH6 4 C5
Churchill Av RH12 34 B6
Churchill Way RH15 29 F4
Churchview Cl RH6 4 C5
Cissbury Cl RH12 35 F3
Cissbury Hill RH11 15 F1
Cissbury Rd RH15 28 C3
Civic Way RH15 28 D4
Clair Ct RH16 24 C5
Clair Rd RH16 24 C5
Clappers Gate RH10 11 G4
Clare Cl RH10 12 C2
Clarence Ct RH16 5 F3
Clarence Dr RH19 21 E6
Clarence Rd RH13 37 E2
Clarence Way RH6 5 F3
Clark Rd RH11 14 D4
Clays Cl RH19 20 D5
Clayton Av BN6 32 B3
Clayton Dr RH15 28 D6
Clayton Hill,
Crawley RH11 15 F1
Clayton Hill,
Hassocks BN6 32 A6
Clayton Pk BN6 32 A2
Clayton Rd BN6 33 E4
Clearwater La RH15 26 B5
Clerks Acre,
Hassocks BN6 32 C2
Clerks Acre,
Hassocks BN6 32 C2
Cleveland Gdns RH15 29 E4
Clevelands RH16 24 C5
Clifton Cl RH6 5 G4
Clifton Rd,
Burgess Hill RH15 28 B2
Clifton Rd,
Crawley RH10 12 D6
Climping Cl RH16 26 B1
Climping Rd RH11 11 E3
Clitherow Gdns RH10 3 C4
Clive Way RH10 12 C5
Clover Ct RH16 24 C6
Cloverfields RH6 5 E3
Cloverlands RH10 12 A3
Clovers End RH12 35 G4
Coachmans Dr RH11 15 E4
Cob Cl RH10 18 D6
Cob Walk RH11 10 D6
Cobbett Cl RH10 12 D3
Cobbetts Mead RH16 27 F1
Cobbles Cres RH10 11 G4
Cobham Way RH10 8 B6
Cobnor Cl RH11 14 C1
Colchins RH15 29 G5
Coldwaltham La RH15 29 G5
Cole Cl RH11 15 E4
Coleridge Cl RH12 35 E3
Colet Rd RH10 15 G3
Colgate Cl RH11 11 E3
College Cl RH19 21 E3
College La,
East Grinstead RH19 21 E3
College La,
Hassocks BN6 31 G2
College Pl BN6 31 G2

College Rd,
Crawley RH10 3 D2
College Rd,
Haywards Heath RH16 24 C4
Collier Row RH10 15 G2
Collingwood Cl,
East Grinstead RH19 21 E6
Collingwood Cl,
Horley RH6 5 E2
Collingwood Cl,
Horsham RH12 34 B5
Collingwood Rd,
Crawley RH10 12 D6
Collingwood Rd,
Horsham RH12 34 B5
Collins Rd RH11 14 B1
Colmer Ct RH15 28 C3
Colmer Pl RH15 28 C3
Colne Walk RH11 14 C1
Colonsay Rd RH11 15 E2
Coltash Rd RH10 12 A6
Coltsfoot Dr RH12 34 D4
Coltsford Cl RH16 26 D2
Colwell Gdns RH16 26 D2
Colwell La,
Haywards Heath RH17 27 E4
Colwell La,
Haywards Heath RH17 27 F2
Colwell Rd RH16 26 D2
Colwyn Cl RH11 14 C2
Combers RH17 17 C5
Commercial Rd RH15 28 C3
Commercial Sq RH16 24 C5
Common La,
Burgess Hill RH15 29 H6
Common La,
Hassocks BN6 33 F1
Compassion Cl RH11 14 B1
Comper Cl RH11 14 B1
Compton Rd RH16 25 F3
Comptons Brow La
RH13 35 F6
Comptons La RH13 35 F5
Condor Way RH15 28 B4
Coney Cft RH12 35 G4
Coney Cl RH11 11 E3
Conifers Cl RH12 35 H3
Coniston Cl,
Crawley RH11 14 A1
Coniston Cl,
Horsham RH12 35 G4
Connaught Gdns RH11 11 G4
Consort Way,
Burgess Hill RH15 28 B5
Consort Way,
Horley RH6 4 D4
Consort Way East RH6 5 E5
Constable Rd RH10 16 A3
Control Tower Rd RH6 7 F3
Cook Rd, Crawley RH10 15 H2
Cook Rd,
Horsham RH12 34 B5
Coolham Ct RH11 10 C5
Coolhurst La RH13 37 H2
Coombe Cl RH11 11 F3
Coombe Hill Rd RH19 20 C6
Coombers La RH16 25 F5
Cooper Row RH10 15 G2
Coopers Cl RH15 29 F1
Cootes Av RH12 34 A6
Copestake Dr RH15 29 G4
Copnall Way RH12 36 D1
Copper Cl RH15 28 A3
Copperfield Pl RH12 34 B5
Copperfields RH13 37 H3
Coppice Rd RH12 35 G4
Coppice Walk RH10 12 B4
Coppice Way RH16 26 B2
Copse Cl, Crawley RH10 18 C6
Copse Cl,
East Grinstead RH19 21 E1
Copse Cl,
Horsham RH12 35 E3
Copse Cres RH11 3 A1
Copse La RH6 5 F3
Copthorne Bank RH10 22 A5
Copthorne Ct RH12 12 B2
Copthorne Rd,
Crawley RH10 13 E3
Copthorne Rd,
Felbridge RH10,19 18 C1
Copthorne Way RH10 13 E1
Copyhold La RH17 23 B6
Copyhold Rd RH19 20 D4
Corby Cl RH11 14 B3
Cornford Cl RH11 14 B3
Cornwall Gdns RH11 21 E5
Coronation Rd RH19 21 E5
Coronet Cl RH10 13 E4
Corselts Cl RH11 14 C2
Corunna Dr RH13 37 F1
Cotswold Cl RH11 11 E5

Cotswold Ct RH13 37 F1
Cottage Cl RH12 35 G3
Cottage Pl RH10 22 D6
Cottingham Av RH12 34 D2
Coltstock Rd RH15 28 A3
County Mall RH10 3 D3
County Oak La RH11 11 G1
County Oak
Retail Pk RH11 11 G1
County Oak Way RH11 11 F1
Court Cl RH11 21 E4
Court Cres RH19 21 E4
Court Lodge Rd RH6 4 B3
Courtlands RH16 26 C1
Courtmead RH17 23 B4
Coverdale Ct*,
Buckhurst Way RH19 20 B2
Covert Cl RH10 11 H4
Cowdray Cl RH10 12 D6
Cowfold Cl RH11 14 C2
Cox Gro RH15 28 C2
Coxcomb Walk RH11 14 D1
Crabbet Rd RH10 12 B4
Crabtree Rd RH11 14 D1
Craigans RH11 10 D6
Cranborne Walk RH10 16 A1
Cranbourne Cl RH6 5 E2
Cranston Rd RH19 20 D3
Cranston Way RH10 18 D5
Craven Rd RH10 16 C1
Crawford Gdns RH13 35 E6
Crawford Way RH19 20 D2
Crawley Av RH10,11 11 E4
Crawley Down Rd RH19 19 F2
Crawley Foyer RH11 3 A2
Crawley La RH10 12 C5
Crawley Rd RH12 35 E5
Crawters Cl RH10 3 F1
Creasys Dr RH11 14 D5
Crescent Cl RH15 29 E4
Crescent Rd,
Burgess Hill RH15 29 E4
Crescent Rd,
East Grinstead RH19 20 C3
Crescent Way,
Burgess Hill RH15 29 E4
Crescent Way,
Horley RH6 5 E4
Crewdson Rd RH6 5 E4
Cricket Ct RH19 20 D2
Cricketfield Rd RH12 36 C2
Cripland Cl RH11 25 F5
Crockham Cl RH11 15 E1
Croft Way RH12 34 A6
Crompton Flds RH10 11 G2
Crompton Way RH10 11 H2
Cromwell Mews RH15 28 C3
Cromwell Pl RH19 21 E5
Cromwell Rd RH15 28 C3
Cross Keys RH19 3 C2
Crossman Ct RH11 15 E4
Crosspath RH10 3 D1
Crossways RH10 12 A5
Crossways Av RH19 20 B3
Crossways Cl RH10 12 A4
Crouchlands Farm RH17 23 B1
Crowberry Cl RH11 14 D3
Crowhurst Cl RH10 13 E5
Croxton La RH16 25 F5
Cuckfield Cl RH11 14 C2
Cuckfield Rd,
Burgess Hill RH15 28 C1
Cuckfield Rd,
Hassocks BN6 31 E2
Cuckmere Cres RH11 10 C6
Culpepper RH15 28 B2
Culross Av RH16 24 B5
Cumbernauld Walk RH11 14 B3
Curf Way RH15 29 F3
Curteys Walk RH11 14 C2
Curzon Av RH12 36 C1
Cuttinglye La RH10 18 C4
Cuttinglye Rd RH10 18 C4
Cyprus Mews RH15 29 E4
Cyprus Rd RH15 29 E4

Dairyfields RH11 10 D6
Dakin Cl RH11 16 D3
Dale Av BN6 32 C3
Dale Cl RH12 35 F4
Dalewood Gdns,
Burgess Hill RH15 29 F4
Dalewood Gdns,
Crawley RH11 12 A3
Dallaway Gdns RH19 20 D4
Dalton Cl RH11 14 D3
Damian Way BN6 32 D2
Danehurst Cres RH13 37 G1
Darenth Way RH6 4 C2
Darleydale RH11 15 F2
Darley Cl RH11 21 E2
Darwin Ct RH12 35 H5
Daux Hill RH12 34 B4
Davis Cl RH11 14 D4

Dawn Rise RH15 22 A
Daynes Way RH15 28 E
De La Warr Rd RH19 21 E
Deanland Rd RH17 17 G
Dedisham Cl RH10 12 E
Deepfields RH6 4 C
Deer Leap RH16 26 A
Deerswood Cl RH11 11 E
Deerswood Ct RH11 11 E
Deerswood Rd RH11 11 E
Delancey Ct RH12 34 C
Delfont Cl RH10 16 C
Delius Gdns RH13 35 H
Dellney Av RH16 27 E
Delta Dr RH6 4 C
Delta Ho*, Delta Dr RH6 4 C
Delting Rd RH11 15 H
Denchers Plat RH11 11 H
Dene Cl RH6 4 E
Dene Tye RH10 12 D
Denham Rd RH15 28 E
Denmans RH10 13 E
Denmans Cl RH16 25 E
Denmans La RH16 25 E
Denne Par RH12 36 D
Denne Rd, Crawley RH11 3 C
Denne Rd,
Horsham RH12 36 D
Departures Rd RH6 7 H
Depot Rd, Crawley RH11 11 G
Depot Rd,
Horsham RH13 3
Derwent Cl,
Crawley RH11 10 C
Derwent Cl,
Haywards Heath RH16 35 G
Devonshire Rd RH13 37 E
Dewar Cl RH11 10 E
Dexter Dr RH19 20 C
Dickens Cl RH19 20 E
Dickens Rd RH10 15 G
Dickins Way RH13 37 G
Dingle Cl RH11 11 E
Dione Walk RH11 11 E
Dirty La RH19 22 C
Discovery Pk RH10 12 B
Ditchling Hill RH11 15 H
Ditchling Rd,
Burgess Hill RH15 29 H
Ditchling Rd,
Haywards Heath RH16 27 E
Dobbins Pl RH11 10 B
Dobson Rd RH11 11 G
Dolby Ter RH6 6 E
Dollis Cl RH10 12 C
Dolphin Rd RH6 24 C
Domewood RH10 18 E
Doncaster Walk RH10 16 A
Donkey La RH6 4 E
Donne Cl RH10 12 C
Donnington Ct RH11 14 C
Doomsday Gdns RH13 37 G
Doomsday La RH13 37 G
Dorking Rd RH12 34 A
Dormans RH11 14 D
Dormans Park Rd RH19 20 C
Dorset Av RH19 20 E
Dorset Ct*, New St RH13 37 E
Dorset Rd RH11 14 C
Dorsten Pl RH11 14 C
Dorsten Sq RH11 14 C
Doubledays RH15 29 E
Dove Cl RH11 11 F
Dovedale Cres RH11 15 E
Dower Walk RH11 10 D
Downe Cl RH6 4 E
Downland Dr RH11 15 E
Downland Pl RH11 15 E
Downs View Rd RH15 28 C
Downs View Rd BN6 32 E
Downscroft RH15 29 E
Downsman Ct RH10 16 E
Downsview BN6 31 E
Downsview Rd RH12 35 G
Downy Lodge RH11 15 G
Drake Cl RH12 35 E
Drake Rd, Crawley RH10 15 G
Drake Rd, Horley RH6 4 E
Drovers Way RH19 29 C
Drummond Cl RH11 26 E
Drummond Rd RH11 14 E
Drummond Rd RH11 14 E
Drury Cl RH10 16 C
Dukes Barn Ct RH16 25
Dukes Rd RH15 25
Dumbrells Court Rd BN6 33 H
Dumbrells Ct BN6 33 E
Dumbrills Cl RH15 29 E
Duncton Cl,
Crawley RH11 11 E
Duncton Cl,
Haywards Heath RH16 26 E
Dunnings Rd RH19 21 E
Dunsfold Cl RH11 10

nstall Av RH15 28 C3
nstall Farm Rd RH15 28 C2
urfold RH12 34 D2
rham CI RH10 15 H3
urkins Rd RH19 20 C2
utchells Copse RH12 35 E3
yall CI RH15 28 B2
yers Almshouses RH10 11 G5

dy CI RH13 37 F2
rles Mdw RH12 35 G3
rlswood CI,
Horsham RH13 35 F5
rlswood CI,
Horsham RH13 35 F5
st End La BN6 33 F3
st Mascalls Rd RH16 25 H5
st Mews RH12 36 D2
st St RH12 36 D2
st Wick RH16 25 G4
stbourne Rd RH19 19 H1
stcroft Mews RH10 36 A2
stdale Rd RH15 29 G3
stern Rd,
Haywards Heath RH16 26 D1
stern Rd,
indfield RH16 25 F4
stgate Mews RH13 37 E2
stway RH6 8 C2
stwood Rd RH10 3 F2
ldington Hill RH11 14 D4
len Rd RH11 14 C1
len Vale RH10 20 C1
gar CI RH10 13 E6
inburgh Way RH19 21 E6
ison PI RH10 3 F3
rich Rd RH11 14 D4
ward Rd RH16 26 C2
ward Way RH15 28 B5
ingham La RH10 22 D4
ingham Rd RH10 18 A1
gar Way RH13 35 H5
ger Way RH10 22 A5
gin CI RH13 35 F6
zabeth Cres RH19 21 E2
zabeth Ct RH6 4 D4
zabethan Way RH10 12 D6
ot CI RH10 16 C1
an Rd RH11 14 C1
n Croft Ct RH10 3 E2
n Dr RH19 21 F4
n Gro RH13 37 F2
ted CI RH11 11 E3
wood CI RH15 28 C6
CI RH10 15 H3
aberwood RH11 11 F3
lyn Rd RH6 4 B3
asworth CI RH10 16 D2
field Rd RH15 15 E3
galee RH19 20 B3
glefield RH12 36 A2
nerdale CI RH11 15 E2
bing Walk RH10 16 A2
som Rd RH10 16 A1
ca Way, Crawley RH10 9 G6
ca Way,
Horsham RH12 34 D4
esson Way RH15 28 B5
dge CI RH10 12 C5
n Way RH15 28 C4
kine CI RH11 14 B3
cots Dr RH19 21 E4
n CI RH10 16 D1
elyn CI RH19 19 G2
elyn Walk RH10 15 G2
ersfield Rd RH13 37 F2
elands RH6 5 F3
hurst CI RH11 11 E5
hurst PI RH11 11 E3
hurst Rd RH11 11 E5
calibur CI RH11 10 B6
change Rd RH10 3 D1
eter CI RH10 15 H3
es CI RH12 34 B5

rbanks RH16 24 D6
rbridge Way RH15 28 D1
field Av RH6 4 D5
field CI RH15 28 C3
field Cres BN6 31 E2
field Gdns RH15 28 C2
urgess Hill RH15 28 C4

st Grinstead RH19 21 E4
tfield Way RH16 24 B3
ford CI RH16 24 D6
lawn CI RH19 20 A3
lawn Dr RH19 20 A3
laws RH6 5 E5
ace La RH15 28 C2
place Hill RH15 28 C2

Fairstone Ct RH6 5 E3
Fairview RH12 34 A6
Fairway,
Copthorne RH10 22 A6
Fairway, Ifield RH11 14 A1
Fairway CI RH10 22 A6
Falcon CI RH11 11 G3
Falklands Dr RH10 35 G5
Fallow Deer CI RH13 35 H6
Fallowfield Way RH6 5 E3
Falmer CI RH13 3 A4
Faraday Ct RH10 11 H1
Faraday Rd RH10 11 H1
Farhalls Cres RH12 35 F4
Farlington Av RH16 24 D5
Farlington CI RH16 24 D5
Farm Av RH12 36 C1
Farm CI, Crawley RH10 12 A4
Farm CI,
East Grinstead RH19 21 F4
Farm CI, Hassocks BN6 32 A2
Farm Cotts RH16 26 A1
Farm La BN6 33 G3
Farm Way RH15 29 G6
Farmleigh CI RH10 12 C3
Farnham Av BN6 32 D1
Farnham CI RH11 15 F6
Farnlea RH15 29 G2
Farr CI RH17 23 C1
Farthings Hill RH12 38 D2
Farthings Walk,
Horsham RH12 36 A1
Farthings Walk,
Horsham RH12 38 D3
Faulkner CI RH11 15 E5
Faulkners Way RH11 15 E2
Fay Rd RH12 34 C4
Felbridge Av RH10 12 D4
Felbridge CI RH19 20 B2
Felbridge Ct RH19 19 H2
Felbridge Rd RH19 19 E2
Felcot Rd RH19 18 D2
Felcourt Rd RH19 20 C1
Fellcott Way RH12 36 A2
Felride RH16 26 C2
Felwater Ct RH19 19 H2
Fenby CI RH13 35 H5
Fenchurch Rd RH10 16 C1
Fenhurst CI RH12 36 A2
Fennel Cres RH11 15 E2
Fermandy La RH10 18 C5
Fern Way RH12 34 D4
Ferndale Rd RH15 29 E5
Ferndown,
Crawley RH10 13 E2
Ferndown, Horley RH6 4 C2
Fernhill CI RH10 18 C5
Fernhill Rd RH6 8 D2
Fernhurst CI RH11 11 E3
Feroners CI RH10 16 B1
Ferring CI RH11 11 E4
Festival Ct RH11 16 D1
Field CI RH15 28 C2
Fieldend RH12 35 G4
Fields End RH16 24 D6
Fieldview RH6 5 E3
Fieldway, Hassocks BN6 33 F3
Fieldway,
Haywards Heath RH16 24 D3
Filbert Cres RH11 10 D6
Filey CI RH11 14 C2
Finches CI RH16 25 F2
Finches Gdns RH16 25 E2
Finches La RH16 25 E2
Finches Park Rd RH16 25 E2
Findon Rd RH11 11 E3
Findon Way RH12 38 B2
Finsbury CI RH11 15 E4
Fir Tree CI RH11 11 E2
Fir Tree Way BN6 32 C2
Firbank Way RH19 20 C4
Firlands,
Haywards Heath RH16 24 D6
Firlands, Horley RH6 5 E3
Firle CI RH10 11 G3
Firtoft CI RH15 29 E3
Fisher CI RH10 15 G1
Fishers Ct RH12 34 C5
Fitchet CI RH11 11 E3
Fitzalan Rd RH13 35 F5
Five Acres RH10 11 G4
Five Oaks Rd RH13 38 A3
Fleming Way RH10 11 G1
Fletcher CI RH10 15 H1
Fletchers CI RH13 37 F2
Flint CI RH11 16 C3
Folders CI RH15 29 G6
Folders Grange RH15 29 F6
Folders La RH15 29 F6
Fontana CI RH10 13 E6
Fontwell Rd RH10 16 A2
Forbes CI RH10 16 C3
Fordingbridge CI RH12 36 C2
Forest CI, Crawley RH10 18 C6

Forest CI,
Horsham RH12 35 G5
Forest Oaks RH13 35 G5
Forest Rd RH12 35 G5
Forest View Rd RH19 20 B6
Forest Vw RH10 16 A2
Forester Rd RH10 15 H2
Forestfield,
Crawley RH10 16 B2
Forestfield,
Horsham RH13 35 F6
Forge CI RH17 38 C1
Forge La, Crawley RH10 12 A4
Forge La,
Horsham RH12 38 C1
Forge PI RH6 4 B6
Forge Way RH15 12 A4
Forge Wood RH10 28 D2
Forge Wood RH10 8 D6
**Forge Wood
Ind Est RH10 8 B6**
Founders La RH16 29 H6
Foundry CI RH13 35 E5
Foundry La RH13 35 E6
Fountains CI RH11 14 D1
Fowler CI RH10 16 C1
Fox CI,
Burgess Hill RH15 28 C5
Fox CI, Crawley RH11 11 E3
Fox Hill RH16 26 C3
Fox Hill RH16 26 D4
Fox Hill Village RH16 26 D4
Foxglove Av RH12 35 E3
Foxglove CI RH15 28 A3
Foxglove Walk RH11 15 E3
Foxhill CI RH10 26 D1
Foxleigh Chase RH12 35 E5
Foxwarren RH16 24 A5
Foxwells RH17 17 C5
Framfield CI RH11 10 D3
Francis Edward Way
RH11 14 B3
Francis Rd RH16 25 F2
Franklands CI RH15 29 E6
Franklands Gdns RH15 29 E6
Franklands Way RH15 29 E6
Franklin Rd RH10 16 C1
Franklynn Rd,
Haywards Heath RH16 26 D1
Franklynn Rd,
Haywards Heath RH16 27 E2
Frankton Av RH16 27 E2
Freeks La RH15 29 E2
French Gdns RH15 25 E4
Freshfield CI RH10 12 B6
Friars CI RH6 32 B2
Friars Oak Rd BN6 32 B1
Friars Rookery RH10 3 E1
Friary Way RH10 3 C3
Friends CI RH11 11 G2
Friston Walk RH11 10 D4
Frith Pk RH19 20 D1
Fry CI RH11 15 E5
Fry Cres RH15 28 C2
Fuel Farm Rd RH6 7 G1
Fulham CI RH11 15 E3
Fulmar CI*,
Fairway RH11 14 A1
Fulmar Dr RH19 21 F2
Furlong Way RH6 8 A1
Furnace Dr RH10 15 H1
Furnace Farm Rd,
Crawley RH10 16 B1
Furnace Farm Rd,
East Grinstead RH19 18 D2
Furnace Par RH10 16 B1
Furnace PI RH10 16 B1
Furze CI RH10 5 G3
Furze La RH19 20 A1
Furzefield RH11 11 E4
Furzefield Rd,
East Grinstead RH19 20 C1
Furzefield Rd,
Horsham RH12 35 H4

Gabriel Rd RH10 16 D3
Gage CI RH10 18 D5
Gainsborough Rd RH10 16 A2
Galahad Rd RH11 10 B6
Gales Dr RH10 3 E1
Gales PI RH10 3 E1
Gander CI RH15 12 A5
Gander Grn RH16 29 E2
Gander Hill RH16 24 D3
Ganymede Ct*,
Arcturus Rd RH11 14 B2
Garden CI RH10 20 D5
Garden House La RH19 20 D5
Garden PI RH12 34 C5
Garden Walk,
Crawley RH11 11 E5
Garden Walk,
Horsham RH12 34 C5
Garden Wood Rd RH19 20 A4

Gardner La RH10 18 B5
Garland Rd RH19 20 C3
Garrett CI RH15 16 D1
Garrick Walk RH11 15 H2
Garton CI RH11 10 B6
Gasson Wood Rd RH11 14 B2
Gateford Dr RH12 35 F3
Gatehouse La RH15 28 A2
Gates CI RH10 16 C3
Gatesmead RH16 24 D2
**Gatwick Bsns Pk
RH6 8 B5**
**Gatwick Gate
Ind Est RH11 7 G4**
**Gatwick International
Distribution Centre
RH10 8 B5**
**Gatwick Metro
Centre RH6 5 E3**
Gatwick Rd RH10 12 A2
Gatwick Way RH6 8 A1
Gemini CI RH11 14 B2
George Pinion CI RH10 34 B6
Georgian CI RH10 12 D6
Gerald CI RH15 29 E4
Gerald Ct RH13 37 F1
Ghyll Cres RH13 37 G3
Gibbons CI RH10 16 D3
Giblets La RH12 35 E2
Giblets Way RH12 35 E2
Giffards CI RH12 36 B1
Gilligan CI RH12 36 B1
Ginhams Rd RH11 11 E5
Gladepoint RH16 24 C6
Gladstone Rd,
Burgess Hill RH15 29 F2
Gladstone Rd,
Horsham RH12 34 D6
Glanville Walk RH11 14 D2
Gleave CI RH19 21 E2
Glebe CI RH10 11 G4
Glebe Rd RH17 23 C3
Glebe Vw RH17 17 C5
Glebelands RH10 18 B6
Glen Vue RH19 20 D4
Glendale CI RH12 35 G3
Glendale Rd RH15 29 F5
Glendon Ho RH10 3 B4
Glendyne CI RH19 21 F5
Glendyne Way RH19 21 F5
Gleneagles CI RH11 3 C4
Glenfield Cotts RH6 6 A2
Glenview CI RH10 11 H3
Gloucester CI RH19 21 E5
Gloucester Rd,
Burgess Hill RH15 28 C4
Gloucester Rd,
Crawley RH10 15 H3
Glovers Rd RH6 6 A2
Goddard CI RH10 16 C3
Godlin Ct RH11 3 C4
Godwin Way RH13 35 F5
Goepel Ct*,
Forge RH10 12 A4
Goffs CI RH11 3 A4
Goffs La RH11 11 E5
Goffs Park Rd RH11 3 A4
Goldcrest CI RH6 4 B3
Golden Hill RH15 29 G3
Goldfinch CI RH11 11 G3
Goldfinch Way RH12 34 C2
Golding CI RH10 12 C6
Goodwin CI RH11 14 C2
Goodwins RH19 20 C1
Goodwood CI RH10 16 A2
Goosegreen CI RH12 34 D4
Gordon CI RH16 24 C4
Gordon Rd,
Burgess Hill RH15 29 F2
Gordon Rd,
Haywards Heath RH16 24 C4
Gordon Rd,
Horsham RH12 34 C5
Goreside La RH17 37 E3
Gorings Mead RH13 37 E3
Gorling CI RH11 10 B6
Gorringes Brook RH12 34 C3
Gorse CI,
Copthorne RH10 22 A6
Gorse CI, Crawley RH11 15 E5
Gorse End RH12 34 D4
Gosden CI RH10 12 B6
Gossops Dr RH11 10 C6
Gossops Green La RH11 10 D6
Goudhurst CI RH10 13 E5
Gower Rd,
Haywards Heath RH16 26 C1
Gower Rd, Horley RH6 4 B4
Grace Ct BN6 32 A1
Grace Rd RH11 14 D4
Graffham CI RH11 11 E3
Granary CI RH6 4 D2
Granary Way RH12 36 A3

Grand Av BN6 32 C2
Grange CI,
Burgess Hill RH15 29 F2
Grange CI,
Crawley RH10 12 A4
Grange Cres RH10 18 C6
Grange Rd RH10 18 B6
Grasmere Gdns RH12 35 G3
Grassmere RH6 5 E3
Grattons Dr RH10 12 C2
Gravelye CI RH16 25 F5
Gravelye La RH16 25 F6
Graveney Rd RH10 12 C6
Gravett Ct RH15 28 D5
Gravetye CI RH10 16 B2
Grays Wood RH6 5 F1
Great Heathmead RH16 24 B5
Greatham Rd RH16 16 C3
Greatlake Ct RH6 5 E3
Grebe Cres RH13 37 H3
Green Hedges Av RH19 20 C3
Green Hedges CI RH19 20 C3
Green La, Crawley RH10 11 H3
Green La,
Crawley Down RH10 18 B2
Green La, Horley RH6 9 F2
Green La, Worth RH10 13 E5
Green Mdws RH16 25 F2
Green Walk RH10 11 H4
Greenacres,
Crawley RH10 12 B6
Greenacres,
Horsham RH12 34 C5
Greenfields CI,
Horley RH6 4 B2
Greenfields CI,
Horsham RH12 35 G3
Greenfields Rd,
Horley RH6 4 C2
Greenfields Rd,
Horsham RH12 35 G4
Greenfields Way RH12 35 F3
Greenfinch Way RH12 34 C2
Greenhill Pk RH17 27 E2
Greenhill Way RH17 27 E2
Greenlands CI RH15 29 E6
Greenlands Dr RH15 29 E6
Greenstede Av RH19 21 E2
Greenway RH12 34 A6
Greenways RH16 24 D4
Greenways Walk RH15 14 F4
Greenwich CI RH11 15 F3
Gregory CI RH10 16 C3
Grendon CI RH6 4 C2
Gresham Walk RH10 15 G3
Grey Alders RH16 25 F4
Greyhound Slip RH10 12 D4
Grier CI RH11 10 B6
Grisedale CI RH11 15 E2
Groombridge Way RH12 36 A2
Grosvenor Rd RH19 20 C4
Grove Rd,
Burgess Hill RH15 29 E4
Grove Rd, Horley RH6 4 C3
Grovelands RH6 5 E5
Grovelands CI RH15 28 D5
Guernsey CI RH11 14 D3
Guildford Rd,
Broadbridge Heath
RH12 38 A1
Guildford Rd,
Horsham RH12 36 B1
Guillemot Path*,
Fairway RH11 14 A1
Guinevere Rd RH11 10 B6
Guinness Ct*,
Woodmans Hill RH11 15 F3
Gunning CI RH11 14 D2
Gwynne Gdns RH19 20 B2

Hackenden CI RH19 20 D2
Hackenden La RH19 20 D2
Hadmans CI RH12 36 D2
Halfacres RH10 11 G4
Halifax CI RH10 13 E2
Halland CI RH10 12 B4
Hallsland RH10 19 E5
Halsford Cft RH19 20 A2
Halsford Grn RH19 20 A2
Halsford La RH19 20 A2
Halsford Park Rd RH19 20 B2
Halton Shaws BN6 31 F4
Hambleton Hill RH11 15 F2
Hambrook RH15 29 F6
Hamilton Rd RH12 34 B6
Hammer Yard RH10 3 B3
Hammerpond Rd RH13 37 G3
Hammerwood Rd RH19 22 B2
Hammond Rd RH11 15 E5
Hammonds Gdns RH15 28 C5
Hammonds Ridge RH15 28 B6
Hampden CI RH12 13 E2
Hampers La RH13 37 G1

Hampshire Ct*, New St RH13 37 E2
Hampton Way RH19 21 E5
Hanbury La RH16 25 E5
Hanbury Rd RH11 10 B6
Handcross Rd RH17 17 A4
Handsworth Ho RH10 3 B4
Hanlye La RH17 23 C1
Hannington Pl BN6 31 E2
Hanover Cl RH10 15 H2
Hanover Rd RH16 26 B1
Hardham Cl RH11 37 E6
Hards Hill RH13 37 E6
Hardy Cl, Crawley RH10 12 C4
Hardy Cl, Horley RH6 4 B4
Hardy Cl, Horsham RH12 34 B6
Hare La RH11 11 E2
Harewood Cl RH10 12 B2
Harlands Cl RH16 24 B4
Harlands Rd RH16 24 B4
Harmans Dr RH19 21 F3
Harmans Mead RH19 21 F4
Harmony Cl RH11 14 B1
Harold Rd RH10 13 E6
Haroldslea Cl RH6 5 F6
Haroldslea Dr RH6 5 F6
Harper Dr RH10 16 C4
Harris Cl RH11 15 E2
Harris Path*, Harris Cl RH11 15 E2
Harrowsley Ct RH6 5 E3
Harrowsley Green La RH6 5 G5
Harting Ct RH11 14 C2
Harvest Cl RH16 25 E3
Harvest Hill RH19 20 D5
Harvest Rd RH10 16 D1
Harvesters, Haywards Heath RH16 26 B3
Harvesters, Horsham RH12 34 D5
Harvey Cl RH11 14 B1
Harwood Rd RH13 35 E6
Harwoods Cl RH19 21 E6
Harwoods La RH19 21 E5
Hascombe Ct RH10 10 D6
Haslett Av East RH10 3 E2
Haslett Av West RH10,11 3 E1
Hassocks Cl RH11 14 C2
Hassocks Rd BN6 31 F4
Hastings Rd RH12 12 C5
Hatchgate RH6 4 C5
Hatchgate Ct RH17 23 C4
Hatchgate La RH17 23 C4
Hatchlands, Haywards Heath RH17 23 C3
Hatchlands, Horsham RH12 35 F2
Hatfield Walk RH11 14 B3
Hathersham La RH6 5 G1
Haven Gdns RH10 18 C5
Havengate RH12 35 E4
Haversham Cl RH10 12 A5
Hawarden Cl RH10 18 D5
Hawkhurst Walk RH10 16 B1
Hawkesbourne Rd RH12 35 F4
Hawkesmoor Rd RH11 14 B1
Hawkins Rd RH12 15 H2
Hawmead RH10 19 E5
Haworth Rd RH10 12 C6
Hawth Av RH10 15 H1
Hawth Cl RH10 15 G1
Hawthorn Cl, Burgess Hill RH15 29 G1
Hawthorn Cl, Crawley RH11 11 F2
Hawthorn Cl, Horsham RH12 34 C5
Hawthorn Pl RH16 26 A3
Haybarn Dr RH12 35 E2
Hayfields RH6 5 E3
Haylind Rd RH16 25 F5
Hayling Ct*, Lundy Cl RH11 15 F3
Haywards Rd RH10 13 E2
Haywards Heath Rd RH17 17 B4
Haywards Rd RH16 26 C2
Hazel Cl, Crawley RH11 11 F3
Hazel Cl, Crawley Down RH10 18 D6
Hazel Gro RH15 29 E5
Hazel Way RH10 18 D5
Hazelgrove Gdns RH16 24 D6
Hazelgrove Rd RH16 24 C6
Hazelhurst RH6 5 F2
Hazelhurst Cres RH12 36 A2
Hazelhurst Dr RH10 13 E6
Hazelwick Av RH10 12 B3
Hazelwick Cl RH10 12 B3
Hazelwick Mill La RH10 12 B3

Hazelwick Rd RH10 12 B4
Hazelwood RH11 10 D6
Hazelwood Cl RH10 18 B5
Headley Cl RH10 13 E2
Heaseawood RH16 26 A2
Heath Cl RH12 38 C2
Heath Rd RH16 24 C6
Heath Rd RH16 24 C6
Heath Sq RH16 24 C5
Heath Way RH10 20 A3
Heathcote Dr RH19 20 A3
Heather Cl, Crawley RH10 22 B6
Heather Cl, Horsham RH12 34 D4
Heather Walk RH11 15 E2
Heatherbank RH16 24 B5
Heatherlands RH16 5 E4
Heathfield RH10 13 E2
Hectors La RH19 22 A1
Hedgeside RH11 15 F4
Hedingham Cl RH6 5 F3
Helicon Ho RH11 3 A3
Hemsby Walk*, Norwich Rd RH10 16 B1
Henbane Ct RH11 15 E3
Henderson Rd RH11 15 E4
Henderson Way RH12 30 A2
Henfield Rd BN6 30 A2
Hengist Cl RH12 16 B2
Henley Dr RH10 16 D2
Henry Burt Way RH15 28 C6
Henshaw Cl RH11 14 C1
Henson Rd RH10 12 B4
Henty Cl RH11 14 B3
Hepplewhite Cl RH11 15 E4
Hereford Cl RH10 15 H3
Heritage Lawn RH6 5 F3
Herm Cl RH11 14 D3
Hermitage La RH19 20 D5
Hermitage Rd RH19 20 D1
Hermits Rd RH10 12 A4
Hernbrook Dr RH13 37 F3
Heron Cl RH11 11 F3
Heron Pl RH19 21 E5
Heron Way RH13 37 G2
Herons Cl RH10 18 C1
Herons Lea RH10 18 B1
Herons Wood Ct RH6 5 E3
Herontye Dr RH19 21 E5
Herrick Cl RH10 12 C3
Hevers Av RH6 4 C5
Hewells Ct RH12 36 D2
Hexham Cl RH10 13 E5
Heyworth Ride RH16 26 A1
Hickling Walk*, Norwich Rd RH10 16 B1
Hickmans Cl RH16 25 F2
Hickmans La RH16 25 E3
Hickstead Ho RH11 15 F2
High Beech La RH16 24 D2
High Oaks RH11 15 E1
High Point RH16 27 E1
High St, Crawley RH10 3 C2
High St, Cuckfield RH17 23 B3
High St, Ditchling BN6 33 F3
High St, East Grinstead RH19 20 D4
High St, Haywards Heath RH16 25 F3
High St, Horley RH6 5 E4
High St, Hurstpierpoint BN6 30 D3
High Trees RH10 24 D6
Highams Hill RH11 10 C6
Highbirch Cl RH11 35 G4
Highdown Ct RH10 16 B2
Highdown Way RH12 35 F3
Highfield Ct RH16 24 C6
Highfield Dr BN6 31 F4
Highfield Rd RH19 20 C2
Highland Ct RH16 24 C6
Highland Rd RH16 26 D2
Highlands Av RH13 37 F1
Highlands Cl BN6 32 C3
Highlands Cres RH13 37 F1
Highlands Dr RH15 28 D3
Highlands Rd RH13 37 F1
Hill Mead RH12 34 A6
Hill Pl RH11 3 A4
Hillary Cl RH19 21 F2
Hillcrest Cl RH10 12 D5
Hillingdale RH11 15 E4
Hillmead RH11 10 C6
Hills Farm La RH12 36 A2
Hills Pl RH12 36 B1
Hillside, Crawley RH10 18 C5
Hillside, Horsham RH12 36 B2
Hillside Cl, Crawley RH11 15 E1
Hillside Cl, East Grinstead RH19 20 D1
Hillside Walk RH16 24 A5
Hillview Gdns RH11 15 F5

Hilton Ct RH6 5 F3
Hindhead Cl RH11 15 F1
Hobbs Field RH13 35 G5
Hobbs Rd RH11 14 D4
Hoblands RH16 27 E1
Hocken Mead RH10 13 E3
Hodgkin Cl RH10 12 C6
Hogarth Rd RH10 15 H3
Holbein Rd RH10 15 H3
Holbrook School La RH12 34 D2
Holder Rd RH10 16 D3
Holders BN6 30 B2
Hollands Field RH12 38 C1
Hollands Way RH19 21 F1
Hollin Ct RH10 11 G2
Hollingbourne Cres RH11 15 F5
Holly Cl, Crawley RH10 12 B4
Holly Cl, Horsham RH12 35 H4
Holly Mews BN6 31 E3
Holly Rd RH16 27 E1
Hollybush Cl RH10 11 H4
Hollybush Rd RH10 11 H4
Hollywood Ct RH16 24 C6
Holman Cl RH11 15 E5
Holmbury Cl RH11 15 F1
Holmbury Keep*, Langshott La RH6 5 F3
Holmbush Cl, Haywards Heath RH16 26 C3
Holmbush Cl, Horsham RH12 34 D4
Holmcroft RH10 3 D4
Holmcroft Cres RH10 15 G1
Holmesdale Rd RH15 28 D6
Holming End RH12 35 G4
Holtye Av RH19 21 E1
Holtye Pl RH19 21 F1
Holtye Rd RH19 21 E3
Holtye Walk RH10 16 B1
Holyrood RH19 21 E5
Holyrood Pl RH11 15 E4
Home Cl RH10 12 C3
Homefield Cl RH6 5 E3
Homestall Rd RH19 22 C1
Homestead La RH11 26 B6
Homethorne Ho RH11 3 B3
Honeysuckle Cl RH6 5 F3
Honeysuckle La RH11 11 F3
Honeysuckle Walk RH12 35 F4
Honeywood Rd RH13 35 G5
Hope Ct RH11 15 E4
Hophurst Cl RH10 18 C5
Hophurst Dr RH10 18 C5
Hophurst Hill RH10 19 E4
Hophurst La RH10 18 C5
Hopkins Ct RH11 15 E4
Horley Rd RH6 6 C3
Horley Row RH6 4 C3
Hornbeam Cl RH13 37 F2
Hornbrook Copse RH13 37 F3
Horndean Cl RH10 13 E2
Horseshoe Cl RH10 13 E4
Horsgate La RH17 23 C3
Horsham By-Pass RH13 34 A5
Horsham By-Pass (North) RH13 34 B2
Horsham Rd RH11 3 A4
Hoskins Pl RH19 21 E1
Hospital Villas RH16 26 D2
Houghton Rd RH10 16 C2
Howard Av RH15 28 B2
Howard Rd, Crawley RH11 14 B3
Howard Rd, Horsham RH15 35 F5
Hoylake Cl RH11 10 A6
Hudson Rd, Crawley RH10 15 H1
Hudson Rd, Haywards Heath RH16 24 C5
Hunstanton Cl RH11 10 A6
Hunter Rd RH11 15 G2
Hunters Mead BN6 30 A3
Huntingdon Way RH12 29 G2
Hurst Av RH12 34 D6
Hurst Cl RH11 14 C1
Hurst Ct RH11 34 D6
Hurst Farm Rd RH19 20 C5
Hurst Gdns BN6 31 E2
Hurst Pk RH12 34 D6
Hurst Rd, Hassocks BN6 31 G5
Hurst Rd, Horley RH6 4 B3
Hurst Rd, Horsham RH12 34 D6
Hurst Wickham Cl BN6 31 G3
Hurstfield Ct RH17 27 E2
Hurstwood La RH17 26 D4
Hutchins Way RH6 4 C2
Hyde Dr RH11 10 B6
Hylands Cl RH10 12 B6

Hyndman Cl RH11 15 E5
Hyperion Ct RH11 14 B2
Hyperion Walk RH6 5 E6
Icklesham Ho RH11 14 C3
Iden Hurst BN6 31 E2
Ifield Av RH11 3 B1
Ifield Dr RH11 10 C4
Ifield Grn RH11 10 D2
Ifield Rd, Crawley RH11 3 A2
Ifield Rd, Horley RH6 6 B5
Ifield St RH11 10 C4
Ifield Wood RH11 10 A2
Imberhorne Bsns Centre RH19 20 A2
Imberhorne La RH19 20 A1
Imberhorne Way RH19 20 A1
Independent Bsns Pk RH19 19 H3
Ingram Cl RH12 36 B1
Inholmes RH10 12 B5
Inholmes Cl RH15 29 F4
Inholmes Park Rd RH15 29 E4
Innes Rd RH12 35 F5
Innovation Dr RH15 28 A4
Institute Walk RH19 20 D4
Iona Cl RH10 15 E2
Iona Way RH10 26 D1
Irving Walk RH10 15 H3
Irwin Dr RH12 36 B1
Isaacs La, Burgess Hill RH15 28 D1
Isaacs La, Haywards Heath RH16 23 D6
Ivanhoe Cl RH11 11 G2
Iveagh Cl RH11 14 D3
Ivory Walk RH11 14 B2
Ivy Dene La RH19 22 B2

Jackdaw Cl RH11 11 F3
Jackdaw La RH12 35 E4
Jackson Rd RH11 15 E5
Jacobean Cl RH10 12 D6
Jacobs Ct RH10 12 C4
James Watt Way RH10 8 B5
Jane Murray Way RH15 28 A3
Janes Cl RH15 29 G2
Janes La RH15 29 F2
Jarvis Cl RH11 15 E5
Jasmine Ct RH12 12 A1
Jenner Rd RH10 12 A1
Jennings Way RH6 5 F4
Jersey Rd RH11 14 D3
Jesters RH15 26 B5
Jewel Walk RH11 14 D2
Jireh Ct RH16 24 C5
Jobes RH17 17 B5
Jockey Mead RH12 36 B3
Johnson Dr RH15 29 H3
Johnson Walk RH10 15 G2
Jolesfield Ct RH11 14 C3
Jordans Cl RH11 11 G3
Jordans Cres RH11 11 G3
Jubilee Rd RH15 28 B5
Jubilee Walk RH10 12 B5
Jubilee Cl RH16 25 E6
Junction Cl RH15 29 F2
Junction Rd RH15 29 E4
Juniper Ct RH16 26 B3
Juniper Rd RH11 11 E2
Jura Cl RH11 15 E2
Juxon Cl RH11 14 C1

Kaithwood Ho RH12 35 G4
Karenza Ct RH13 34 D6
Keats Cl RH16 35 E2
Keats Pl RH19 20 C4
Keble Cl RH10 12 D2
Kelmscott Rise RH11 15 E5
Kelsey Cl RH6 4 C4
Kelsey Ct RH15 29 G3
Kelso Cl RH10 13 E5
Kelvin Bsns Centre RH10 12 A2
Kelvin La RH10 11 H1
Kelvin Way RH10 11 H2
Kemps BN6 30 D2
Kempshott Rd RH12 34 B5
Kempton Rd RH11 15 F2
Kendal Cl RH10 16 D3
Kendall Ct RH16 26 D2
Kenilworth Cl RH11 15 E3
Kenmara Cl RH10 12 B2
Kenmara Ct RH10 12 B1
Kennedy Av RH19 20 C2
Kennedy Rd RH13 37 E2
Kennel La RH6 4 A5
Kennet Cl RH11 10 C6
Kensington Rd RH11 15 E4
Kent Ct*, New St RH13 37 E2
Kents Rd RH16 26 D1
Kentwyns Dr RH13 37 F3
Kenya Ct RH6 4 C3
Kerves La RH13 37 F4

Kestrel Cl, Crawley RH11 11
Kestrel Cl, Horsham RH12 35
Keswick Cl RH11 14
Keymer Cl RH15 29
Keymer Gdns RH15 29
Keymer Par RH15 29
Keymer Pk RH16 32
Keymer Rd, Burgess Hill RH15 29
Keymer Rd, Crawley RH11 3
Keymer Rd, Hassocks BN6 32
Kidborough Rd RH11 14
Kidbrook RH16 25
Kidmans Cl RH12 29
Kidworth Cl RH6 4
Kilbarn Ct RH16 25
Kiln Cl RH10 18
Kiln La, Haywards Heath RH16 29
Kiln La, Horley RH6 4
Kiln Rd RH10 18
Kilnbarn Way RH16 26
Kilnmead RH10 3
Kilnmead Cl RH10 3
Kimberley Cl RH6 4
Kimberley Rd RH10 12
Kindersley Cl RH19 21
King George Av RH19 21
King St RH19 20
Kingfisher Cl RH10 12
Kingfisher Rise RH19 21
Kingfisher Way RH12 34
Kings Copse RH19 21
Kings Ct RH13 35
Kings Dr BN6 32
Kings Mews RH12 36
Kings Rd, Haywards Heath RH16 26
Kings Rd, Horley RH6 4
Kings Rd, Horsham RH12 35
Kings Ride RH15 29
Kings Way RH15 29
Kingsate RH12 35
Kingscote Hill RH11 15
Kingslea RH13 35
Kingsley Cl RH6 4
Kingsley Rd, Crawley RH11 14
Kingsley Rd, Horley RH6 4
Kingsmead Cl RH12 35
Kingsmead Pl RH12 38
Kingsmead Rd RH12 35
Kingswood Cl RH11 15
Kipling Cl RH10 15
Kipling Ct RH16 24
Kipling Way RH19 20
Kirdford Cl, Burgess Hill RH15 29
Kirdford Cl, Crawley RH11 10
Kites Cl RH11 3
Kithurst Ct RH11 15
Kitsmead RH10 22
Kittiwake Cl RH11 14
Knepp Cl RH10 12
Knighton Cl RH10 12
Knoll Pl RH16 25
Knowle Cl RH10 22
Knowle Dr RH10 22
Knowle Gro RH19 22
Knyveton Ct RH15 29
Kymer Gdns BN6 32

Laburnum Way RH16 27
Ladbroke Rd RH6 5
Lady Margaret Rd RH11 10
Lady Margaret Walk*, Lady Margaret Rd RH11 10
Ladymead RH15 10
Ladymead Cl RH10 16
Lagwood Cl BN6 30
Lake La RH6 5
Lake View Rd RH19 18
Laker Ct RH10 12
Lakeside RH12 34
Lamberhurst Walk RH10 16
Lambeth Cl RH11 15
Lambeth Walk RH11 15
Lambourn Cl RH19 20
Lambourne Cl RH10 16
Lambs Cres RH12 35
Lambs Farm Cl RH12 35
Lambs Farm Rd RH12 35
Lambyn Cft*, Oakside La RH6 5
Lanark Ct RH16 37
Lancaster Cl RH11 37
Lancaster Dr RH19 21

ancelot CI RH11 10 B6
ancing CI RH11 10 D4
ancing Ct RH12 35 G5
anden Pk RH6 4 B2
ane Hurst Gdns RH10 12 C3
anercost Rd RH11 3 A4
angdale Rd RH11 14 A1
anghurstwood Rd RH12 34 C1
angley Ct RH10 12 A3
angley Dr RH11 11 F3
angley La RH11 10 D3
angley Par RH11 11 F3
angley Pl RH11 11 F2
angley Walk RH11 11 E2
angridge Ct RH16 25 E6
angridge Dr RH19 20 C5
angridge Way RH15 28 C2
angshott RH6 5 E2
angshott La RH6 5 E3
angstone CI RH10 16 D2
ansbury Rd RH11 15 E4
ansdown Ct RH11 35 G3
anyon CI RH12 35 F3
anyon Mews RH12 35 F3
apwing RH13 35 F6
arch End RH12 34 B6
arch Way RH16 25 F6
arches Way RH10 18 D5
ark Rise RH11 11 E3
arkfield Rd RH6 5 E3
arkins Rd RH6 7 F2
ashmere RH10 22 C5
aski Ct RH11 15 E4
atimer CI RH11 11 G2
aud Dr RH10 12 D6
aughton Rd RH12 35 F4
aurel CI, Burgess Hill RH15 29 G1
aurel CI, Crawley RH10 16 B2
aurel Dene RH19 21 E4
aurel Walk RH13 37 F2
avant CI RH11 14 C1
avington Ct RH11 10 C4
awrie La RH16 25 F5
aws CI RH11 10 B6
awson Hunt nd Pk RH12 38 B1
ea CI RH11 4 D3
ea CI RH11 14 C1
eacroft RH12 20 C3
echford Rd RH6 4 D6
edgers Mdw RH17 23 B3
ie St RH6 4 B4
echpool La RH13 35 G5
ggyfield Ct RH12 34 B4
icester Ct RH10 13 E5
ighlands RH10 12 C3
ith View Rd RH12 35 F2
onard Way RH12 37 F1
onardslee Ct RH10 16 B2
opold Rd RH11 11 F5
tchworth Ct RH11 14 B3
veret La RH11 11 E3
wes Rd RH10 12 D6
wes Rd, East Grinstead RH19 21 E4
wes Rd, Hassocks BN6 33 F3
wes Rd, Haywards Heath RH16 25 F3
wisham Ct RH11 15 E3
yfield BN6 30 B3
ylands Pk RH15 29 E2
ylands Rd RH15 28 D3
yton Lea RH17 23 B3
dsey CI RH10 16 D2
llywhite CI RH15 28 C2
me Av RH12 35 F5
me CI, Copthorne RH10 22 B5
me CI, Crawley RH11 11 E2
me Tree Gro RH16 25 G4
mes Av RH6 5 E5
nchmere Pl RH11 10 D4
ncoln CI, Crawley RH10 15 H3
ncoln CI, Horley RH6 4 D5
ncoln Wood RH16 24 A5
nden Av RH19 20 B3
nden CI, Crawley RH10 16 B2
nden CI, Horsham RH12 35 E5
nden Gro RH16 25 F4
ndfield Ent Pk RH16 25 G4
ngfield Dr RH10 13 E5
ngfield CI RH11 20 C1
nnell CI RH11 15 E6
ntott Gdns RH15 15 E2
nsmore Cres RH11 15 E2
ttle Bentswood RH16 25 E5

Little Bentswood CI RH16 24 D5
Little Black Hill RH16 25 F3
Little Comptons RH13 37 G2
Little Copse Rd BN6 32 B1
Little Crabtree RH11 11 F4
Little Grebe RH12 34 C4
Little Hatch RH12 35 E4
Little Haven La RH12 35 F4
Little Park La BN6 31 E3
Livingstone Rd, Burgess Hill RH15 28 C4
Livingstone Rd, Crawley RH10 15 H1
Livingstone Rd, Horsham RH13 37 E2
Lloyds Ct RH10 11 H2
Lockhart Ct RH16 26 D2
Lockwood CI RH12 35 G4
Lockwood Ct RH10 12 A3
Lodge CI, Crawley RH11 11 F5
Lodge CI, East Grinstead RH19 20 B4
Lodge Hill La BN6 33 F2
Lodge La BN6 32 D3
London La RH17 23 B3
London Rd, Balcombe RH17 17 B4
London Rd, Burgess Hill RH15 28 D4
London Rd, Crawley RH10 11 G4
London Rd, Cuckfield RH17 23 B2
London Rd, East Grinstead RH19 20 A1
London Rd, Hassocks BN6 33 A2
London Rd, Horley RH6 4 C6
London Rd, Horsham RH12 36 D1
Long Acre RH10 18 C5
Long CI RH10 12 D5
Long Park Corner BN6 33 F4
Longacre Cres RH17 23 C2
Longbridge Rd RH6 4 C6
Longbridge Walk RH6 4 C6
Longbridge Way RH6 4 C6
Longchamp CI*, Carlton Tye RH6 5 F4
Longfellow CI RH12 35 E2
Longfield Rd RH12 36 B3
Longhurst RH15 29 G5
Longmere Rd RH11 14 D4
Longmere Rd RH10 11 G4
Longwood Vw RH10 16 B2
Loppets Rd RH10 16 A2
Loriners RH10 15 G2
Lovetofts RH11 10 D6
Lowdells CI RH19 20 B1
Lowdells Dr RH19 20 B1
Lowdells La RH19 20 A1
Lowe CI RH11 15 E5
Lower Barn CI RH12 35 E4
Lower Church Rd RH15 28 D4
Lower Dene RH19 21 E4
Lower Mere RH19 21 E5
Lower Tanbridge Way RH12 36 C2
Lower Village RH16 26 A3
Lowestoft Walk RH10 16 B2
Lowfield Heath Rd RH6 6 C3
Lowfield Rd RH16 26 D2
Lowfield Way RH11 7 H5
Lowlands Rd RH11 15 E2
Loxwood Walk RH11 10 C4
Lucas CI RH19 21 E4
Lucas Grange RH16 24 B5
Lucas Way RH10 16 B2
Lucastes Av RH16 24 B4
Lucastes La RH16 24 A5
Lucastes Rd RH16 24 A6
Lucerne Dr RH10 16 D2
Lulworth CI RH11 14 D2
Lumley Ct RH6 4 D3
Lumley Rd RH6 4 D3
Lunchmere Ho RH11 10 D4
Lundy CI RH11 15 F3
Lurgashall RH15 29 G5
Lutyens CI RH11 14 B2
Luxford CI RH12 35 F4
Luxford Rd RH19 25 F3
Luxfords La RH19 22 A2
Lyndhurst CI RH11 3 B4
Lynton CI, East Grinstead RH19 21 E2
Lynton CI, Hassocks BN6 31 F4
Lynton Park Av RH19 21 E3
Lynwood Ct RH12 34 C6
Lyon CI RH10 16 D3
Lyon CI RH13 37 F1
Lyoth La RH16 25 F6

Lyric CI RH10 16 D1
Lytton Dr RH10 13 E4

Mackie Av BN6 32 C2
Macleod Rd RH13 37 F2
Maddox Dr RH10 13 E6
Madehurst Ct RH11 14 C2
Madeira Way RH12 36 D1
Magdalene Rd RH10 12 C2
Magnolia Ct RH6 4 D4
Magpie La RH13 37 G6
Magpie Walk RH10 12 A3
Maiden La RH11 11 E3
Maidenbower Dr RH10 16 C1
Maidenbower Dr RH10 16 C1
Maidenbower La RH10 16 D1
Maidenbower Pl RH10 16 D1
Maidenbower Sq RH10 16 D1
Maize Cft RH6 5 E3
Malcolm Gdns RH6 4 A6
Mallard CI, Horley RH6 4 D2
Mallard CI, Horsham RH12 34 C4
Mallard Pl RH19 21 E5
Mallow CI RH12 35 E3
Malthouse La RH15 28 A3
Malthouse Rd RH10 3 C4
Malvern Rd RH11 3 A4
Manaton Ct RH16 26 D1
Mann CI RH11 15 E5
Manning CI RH19 20 C2
Mannings CI RH10 12 D2
Manor Av BN6 32 C1
Manor CI, Burgess Hill RH15 29 G3
Manor CI, Horley RH6 4 C4
Manor Dr, Haywards Heath RH17 23 B2
Manor Dr, Horley RH6 4 C4
Manor Flds RH13 35 G5
Manor Gdns BN6 31 E3
Manor La RH13 37 H3
Manor Rd, Burgess Hill RH15 29 G2
Manor Rd, East Grinstead RH19 20 B3
Manor Rd, Hassocks BN6 31 E3
Manor Rd, Horsham RH12 35 F4
Manor Royal RH10 11 H2
Manor Royal Ind Trading Est RH10 11 H2
Manorfields RH11 14 A3
Mansell Ct RH15 29 F4
Mansion Ct RH15 29 G4
Maple CI, Burgess Hill RH15 29 F4
Maple CI, Crawley RH11 11 F2
Maple CI, Haywards Heath RH16 27 F1
Maple CI, Horsham RH12 35 G4
Maple Dr, Burgess Hill RH15 28 D2
Maple Dr, East Grinstead RH19 21 F4
Maple Grn RH11 3 A4
Marchants CI BN6 31 E3
Marchants Rd BN6 31 E3
Marchants Way RH15 28 D1
Marion Rd RH10 16 B2
Market Pl, Burgess Hill RH15 29 E4
Market Pl, Haywards Heath RH16 24 C5
Market Sq RH12 36 D2
Marlborough CI, Crawley RH11 15 F4
Marlborough CI, Horsham RH12 35 G4
Marlborough Dr RH15 29 F4
Marle Av RH15 28 D2
Marlow Ct RH10 11 G4
Marlow Dr RH16 25 F6
Marlpit CI RH19 20 C1
Marsh Ct RH11 15 E4
Marshall Rd RH10 16 D1
Martin CI RH11 11 F3
Martletts Ct RH12 34 C4
Martyns Pl RH19 21 E5
Martyrs Av RH11 11 F2
Marvell CI RH10 12 C3
Marylands Rd RH11 24 D6
Masefield Rd RH11 14 B3
Mason CI RH19 20 D3
Mason Rd RH10 15 G2
Massetts Rd RH6 4 C5
Matthews Dr RH10 16 C3
Matthey Pl RH10 13 E3
Maunsell Pk RH10 12 C5
Maxton Walk RH11 15 E4
Maxwell Way RH10 12 A2
Mayes CI RH10 16 C1

Mayfield RH10 13 E5
Mayfield Ct RH15 29 F4
Mayflower CI RH10 12 D6
Mayflower Rd RH16 24 D6
Mayflower Rd RH16 24 D6
Mayhouse Rd RH15 28 C5
Maynard Ct RH11 22 C5
Maypole Rd, Ashurst Wood RH19 22 C2
Maypole Rd, East Grinstead RH19 20 C3
McIndoe Rd RH19 20 C2
McIver CI RH19 19 G2
Mead Rd RH10 11 H4
Meadow App RH10 22 A5
Meadow CI, Crawley RH10 22 A5
Meadow CI, Haywards Heath RH17 17 C5
Meadow CI, Horsham RH12 35 G4
Meadow Dr RH16 25 F4
Meadow Farm La RH12 35 E2
Meadow La, Burgess Hill RH15 28 D6
Meadow La, Haywards Heath RH16 25 F4
Meadowbrook Ind Est RH10 12 B2
Meadowcroft CI, Crawley RH10 10 C6
Meadowcroft CI, East Grinstead RH19 20 B3
Meadowcroft CI, Horley RH6 8 C1
Meadowlands RH11 11 E5
Meadowside RH6 5 E3
Meadowside*, Oatlands RH6 5 E3
Meadvale RH12 36 A1
Meath Green Av RH6 4 C2
Meath Green La RH6 4 B1
Medlar CI RH11 11 F2
Medway Ct RH12 35 H4
Medway Rd RH11 10 C6
Medwin Walk RH12 36 D1
Medwin Way RH12 36 D1
Meeds Rd RH15 28 D5
Melbourne Way RH12 35 F5
Melksham Ct RH13 37 F2
Mendip Walk RH11 11 E5
Mercer CI RH10 16 C3
Mercury CI RH11 14 B2
Mereworth Dr RH10 12 D4
Meridan Way RH19 21 E2
Meridian CI RH11 14 C3
Meridian Gro RH6 5 F3
Merlin CI RH11 10 B5
Merlin Way RH19 21 F2
Merryfield Dr RH12 34 A6
Merton Rd RH11 15 E5
Metcalf Way RH11 11 G1
Michael Cres RH6 4 D6
Michelbourne CI RH15 28 B6
Michell CI RH12 36 B1
Middle St RH12 36 D2
Middle Village RH16 26 A2
Middle Way RH15 29 E4
Middlefield RH6 5 F3
Middleton Rd RH12 36 B1
Middleton Way RH11 10 B6
Midfields RH15 29 E3
Midfields Dr RH15 29 E3
Midfields Walk RH15 29 E3
Midgeley Rd RH10 11 H3
Midhurst CI RH11 10 D4
Milborne Rd RH10 16 C4
Mill Bay La RH12 36 C2
Mill CI, East Grinstead RH19 20 D6
Mill CI, Horley RH6 4 B3
Mill Cotts RH10 20 D6
Mill Green Rd RH16 24 C4
Mill Hill CI RH16 24 C3
Mill La, Crawley RH10 10 D3
Mill La, East Grinstead RH19 19 F1
Mill La, Haywards Heath RH17 17 C5
Mill La, Horley RH6 4 A4
Mill La, Ifield RH10 18 A2
Mill Rd, Burgess Hill RH15 29 E2
Mill Rd, Crawley RH10 12 B4
Mill Stream Mdw RH10 24 C4
Mill Way RH19 20 D6
Millais RH13 35 F6
Millais CI RH11 14 C3
Millais Ct RH13 35 G6
Millbank RH15 29 E2
Millers Gate RH15 28 C4
Millers Way RH15 29 E3
Mills CI RH13 37 G2
Millthorpe Rd RH12 35 F5

Millwood RH15 29 E3
Milne CI RH11 14 B2
Milnwood Rd RH12 34 C6
Milton Cres RH19 20 B4
Milton CI RH16 24 C5
Milton Mount Av RH10 12 D4
Milton Rd, Crawley RH10 12 C4
Milton Rd, Haywards Heath RH16 24 C5
Milton Rd, Horsham RH12 34 B6
Mindleheim Av RH19 21 F3
Miranda Walk RH11 14 B2
Mistley Gdns RH6 4 A6
Mitchells Rd RH10 3 F2
Mitford Walk RH11 14 D2
Moat Rd RH19 20 D3
Moat Walk RH10 12 D5
Mocatta Way RH15 28 B2
Mole CI RH11 11 E3
Molins Ct*, Breezehurst Dr RH11 14 D3
Monarch CI RH11 14 D2
Monksfield RH10 3 F1
Montreux Ct*, Mendip Walk RH11 11 E5
Moons La RH13 37 E2
Moor Park Cres RH11 10 A6
Moor Pl RH19 20 C3
Moorcroft CI RH11 11 E5
Moore Ct RH12 36 B2
Moorhead Rd RH12 35 H4
Moorland Rd RH10 16 D2
Morecombe CI RH11 14 C1
Morrell Av RH12 35 F4
Morrison CI RH11 15 E4
Morth Gdns RH12 36 D2
Morton CI RH11 15 E5
Morton Rd RH19 20 D6
Mosford CI RH6 4 C2
Mount CI RH10 12 D4
Mountbatten CI RH11 15 F3
Mowbray Dr RH11 14 C1
Moyne Rd RH11 15 E3
Muirfield CI RH11 10 A6
Mulberry CI RH12 34 C4
Mulberry Gdns RH12 38 C2
Mulberry La BN6 33 F3
Mulberry Rd RH11 11 E2
Mullein Walk RH11 14 D3
Munns Dr RH15 29 E2
Murray Ct RH13 35 G5
Musgrave Av RH19 20 D5
Muster Ct RH16 24 B6
Muster Grn North RH16 24 B6
Muster Grn South RH16 24 B6
Mytten Bank RH17 23 B3
Mytten CI RH17 23 B3

Naldrett CI RH12 35 E5
Napier Way RH10 12 A2
Nash Rd RH10 15 H2
Neale CI RH19 20 A1
Needles CI RH12 36 B2
Nelson CI RH10 16 D1
Nelson Rd RH12 34 B6
Neptune CI RH11 14 B2
Nesbit Ct RH11 14 B2
Netherwood RH11 15 E2
Netley CI RH11 15 F6
Neville CI RH11 14 D2
Neville Cotts Rd RH16 33 F4
New England Rd RH16 24 C4
New Moorhead Dr RH12 35 H3
New Rd BN6 32 A5
New St, Crawley RH10 12 B5
New St, Horsham RH13 37 E2
New Way La BN6 31 F4
Newark Rd RH10 11 H4
Newbridge CI RH12 38 A2
Newbury La RH17 23 B4
Newbury Rd RH10 13 E5
Newlands RH17 17 B5
Newlands CI, Hassocks BN6 32 D2
Newlands CI, Horley RH6 4 C2
Newlands Cres RH10 20 C3
Newlands Pk RH10 18 A2
Newlands Rd, Crawley RH10 3 A3
Newlands Rd, Horsham RH12 34 C5
Newman CI RH10 16 C1
Newmarket Rd RH10 16 A2
Newport CI RH15 28 C3
Newstead Hall RH6 5 F5
Newton CI RH16 25 F3
Newton CI RH16 24 C5
Newton Rd, Crawley RH10 12 A1

Newton Rd,
Haywards Heath RH16 25 F3
Nightingale Cl,
Crawley RH11 11 E3
Nightingale Cl,
East Grinstead RH19 20 C6
Nightingale
Ind Est RH12 34 D6
Nightingale La RH15 28 D6
Nightingale Rd RH10 36 D2
Nightingales Cl RH13 37 G1
Ninfield Ct RH11 14 C3
Niven Cl RH10 13 E6
Noahs Ark La RH16 25 F4
Noel Grn RH15 29 E2
Noel Rise RH15 29 E3
Norfolk Cl,
Crawley RH11 14 B3
Norfolk Cl, Horley RH6 4 C5
Norfolk Ct RH12 35 H4
Norfolk Ter RH12 37 E1
Norman Rd RH15 28 D4
Normandy RH12 36 D2
Normandy Cl,
Crawley RH10 16 C1
Normandy Cl,
East Grinstead RH19 21 E5
Normandy Gdns RH12 36 D2
Normanhurst Rd RH10 12 A5
North Bank BN6 32 A2
North Cl RH10 11 H4
North Ct BN6 32 A2
North End BN6 33 F3
North Heath Cl RH10 34 D4
North Heath
Ind Est RH12 34 D3
North Heath La RH12 34 D5
North Holmes Cl RH12 35 G4
North Mead RH10 11 H3
North Par RH12 34 A4
North Rd, Crawley RH10 12 A4
North Rd,
Haywards Heath RH16 25 E6
North St RH12 37 E1
North Terminal Approach Rd
RH6 8 A1
North Way RH6 8 A1
Northdown Cl RH12 35 F5
Northdown Ter*,
Dormans Park Rd RH19 20 B2
Northern Breach RH17 23 B3
Northgate Av RH10 3 E1
Northgate Pl RH10 11 H4
Northgate Rd RH10 3 C1
Northlands Av RH16 25 F6
Northlands Rd RH12 35 E2
Northway RH15 29 G3
Northwood Pk,
Crawley RH10 12 B1
Northwood Pk,
Crawley RH10 12 B1
Norwich Rd RH10 3 C1
Norwood Hill Rd RH6 6 B2
Nursery Cl,
Hassocks BN6 31 E2
Nursery Cl,
Haywards Heath RH16 24 B6
Nursery La RH6 4 A5
Nurserylands RH11 10 D6
Nuthatch Way RH12 34 D2
Nuthurst Ct RH11 10 D4
Nye La BN6 33 G4
Nye Rd RH15 29 F3
Nymans Cl RH12 35 F2
Nymans Ct RH10 16 B2

Oak Bank RH16 24 D3
Oak Cl RH10 22 A5
Oak Croft RH19 21 F5
Oak Dell RH10 12 D4
Oak Hall Pk RH15 29 E6
Oak La RH12 38 C2
Oak Rd RH11 3 A3
Oak Tree Way RH13 35 F6
Oakapple Cl RH11 15 E5
Oakdale Rd RH16 27 E1
Oakenfield RH15 28 D2
Oakfield Cl RH16 25 E3
Oakfield Way RH19 20 D2
Oakfields RH10 12 D4
Oakhaven RH10 15 G1
Oakhill Rd RH13 37 E1
Oakhurst RH16 24 C3
Oakhurst Gdns RH19 20 A3
Oakhurst La RH16 24 C3
Oakhurst Mews RH13 35 G5
Oaklands 5 F3
Oaklands Cl RH13 37 F1
Oaklands Rd RH16 24 B5
Oakleigh Rd RH12 35 F5
Oakley Cl RH19 21 G5
Oakmead Rd RH15 28 C6
Oakroyd Cl RH15 29 G1

Oaks Cl RH12 35 G3
Oakside Ct RH6 5 F3
Oakside La RH6 5 F3
Oakway RH10 11 G4
Oakwood RH15 29 F4
Oakwood
Ind Est RH10 12 B2
Oakwood Rd,
Burgess Hill RH15 29 E4
Oakwood Rd,
Haywards Heath RH16 24 B6
Oakwood Rd,
Horley RH6 4 D3
Oates Walk RH10 15 H2
Oathall Av RH16 24 D5
Oathall Rd RH16 24 C6
Oatlands, Crawley RH11 10 D6
Oatlands, Horley RH6 5 E3
Oberon Way RH11 14 B2
Ockenden La RH17 23 B4
Ockenden Way BN6 32 B3
Ockley La BN6 32 D3
Ockley Way BN6 32 D2
Old Barn Cl RH16 7 H3
Old Brighton Rd RH11 2 H5
Old Control Tower Rd
RH6 7 F3
Old Crawley Rd RH12 35 H3
Old Denne Gdns RH12 36 D2
Old Farm Cl RH17 27 E2
Old Guildford Rd RH12 38 B1
Old Holbrook RH12 35 E1
Old Hollow RH10 13 F5
Old Horsham Rd RH11 15 E1
Old Manor Cl RH11 10 D3
Old Martyrs*,
Martyrs Av RH11 11 G2
Old Millmeads RH12 34 C4
Old Orchards RH10 13 E6
Old Park Cl RH17 23 C4
Old Rd RH19 21 E4
Old School Cl RH16 25 F3
Old School Pl RH15 28 D5
Old Station Cl RH10 18 C6
Old Wickham La RH16 24 C3
Old Wickhurst La RH12 38 C3
Oldbury Cl RH12 35 G2
Oldfield Cl RH16 4 C6
Oldfield Rd RH6 4 C6
Oldlands Av,
Hassocks BN6 32 D2
Oldlands Av,
Haywards Heath RH17 17 B6
Oliver Rd RH12 36 B3
Olivier Rd RH10 17 E1
Onslow Ct RH10 12 B2
Orchard Cl,
Haywards Heath RH16 24 C2
Orchard Cl, Horley RH6 4 C3
Orchard Corner RH16 25 F5
Orchard Cotts RH17 23 B3
Orchard Cotts*,
Chapel Rd RH10 6 C2
Orchard La,
Ditchling BN6 33 F1
Orchard La,
Hassocks BN6 32 C2
Orchard Rd,
Burgess Hill RH15 28 B4
Orchard Rd,
Horsham RH13 37 F2
Orchard St RH11 3 B2
Orchard Way,
Burgess Hill RH15 28 C4
Orchard Way,
East Grinstead RH19 20 C4
Orchard Way,
Hassocks BN6 30 D3
Orchard Way,
Haywards Heath RH16 24 B2
Orchid Pk RH16 27 G1
Orde Cl RH10 12 D2
Oriel Cl RH12 12 C2
Orion Cl RH11 14 A2
Orion Par BN6 32 C3
Ormerod Ct RH16 24 C6
Ormesbury Walk*,
Norwich Rd RH10 16 B1
Osmund Cl RH10 13 E6
Osney Cl RH11 3 A4
Otford Cl RH11 15 F5
Ottafield Ct RH16 24 B6
Otway Cl RH11 14 C2
Oulton Walk*,
Norwich Rd RH10 16 B1
Overdene Dr RH11 10 D5
Overton Shaw RH19 20 D1
Owen Cl RH15 28 C5
Owers Cl RH13 37 F1
Owlbeech Pl RH13 35 H5
Owlbeech Way RH13 35 H5
Owlcastle Cl RH12 34 D4
Owletts RH10 12 D1

Oxford Rd,
Crawley RH10 15 H3
Oxford Rd,
Horsham RH13 37 E1

Packer Cl RH19 21 E1
Packham Way RH15 28 D2
Paddock Gdns RH19 20 D6
Paddockhall Rd RH16 24 B6
Paddockhurst Rd RH11 10 C6
Padstow Walk RH11 14 B2
Padwick Rd RH13 37 G1
Paget Cl RH13 37 F3
Pagewood Cl RH10 17 E2
Pallingham Dr RH10 16 C3
Palmer Cl RH6 4 C1
Palmer Rd RH10 16 C3
Pangdene Cl RH15 28 C6
Pannell Cl RH19 20 C4
Pannett RH15 28 B2
Parham Rd RH11 10 C4
Parish Ho RH11 3 B4
Park Av BN6 32 D4
Park Cl,
Burgess Hill RH15 28 D3
Park Cl, Hassocks BN6 31 E3
Park Cl,
Burgess Hill RH15 28 D3
Park Ct,
Haywards Heath RH16 24 C6
Park East RH16 26 D2
Park Farm Cl RH11 34 D2
Park Farm Rd RH12 34 D2
Park La,
East Grinstead RH19 22 B2
Park La,
Haywards Heath RH16 25 G1
Park Pl RH12 36 D2
Park Rd,
Burgess Hill RH15 28 D3
Park Rd,
East Grinstead RH19 20 C3
Park Rd,
Haywards Heath RH16 24 C1
Park Rise RH12 34 B5
Park St RH12 36 D1
Park Ter West RH12 36 D1
Park Ter RH13 37 E2
Park View Gdns RH19 20 C1
Park Vw, Crawley RH11 11 F6
Park Vw,
Haywards Heath RH16 24 C5
Park Vw, Horley RH6 4 D4
Park Way RH12 36 D2
Park West RH16 26 D2
Parker Cl RH10 16 D1
Parkfield RH12 34 C6
Parkfield Cl RH11 10 C6
Parkfield Way RH16 26 A1
Parkhurst Gro RH6 4 C3
Parkhurst Rd RH6 4 B3
Parklands Rd RH6 32 B3
Parklawn Av RH6 4 C2
Parkside, Crawley RH10 3 D2
Parkside,
East Grinstead RH19 20 B4
Parkside, Hassocks BN6 32 C2
Parkside Mews RH12 37 E1
Parkview BN6 31 E4
Parkway, Crawley RH10 12 C3
Parkway, Horley RH6 4 D4
Parnell Cl RH10 16 D1
Parry Cl RH13 35 H5
Parsonage
Bsns Pk RH12 35 E5
Parsonage Rd RH12 34 D5
Parsonage Way RH12 35 E5
Parsons Cl RH6 4 B3
Parsons Walk RH12 36 A3
Parthings La RH13 36 A3
Pasture Hill Rd RH16 24 B4
Patching Cl RH11 10 C4
Patchings RH13 37 G1
Path Link RH10 3 E1
Patrington Cl RH11 14 D2
Patterdale RH11 15 E2
Pavilion Cl BN6 32 A1
Pavilion Way RH19 20 D1
Pax Cl RH11 14 B1
Payne Cl RH10 16 D1
Payton Dr RH15 28 C5
Peacemaker Cl RH11 14 D1
Peacock Walk RH11 14 D2
Pear Tree Cl RH15 28 C4
Pearson Rd RH10 12 C5
Peary Cl RH12 34 D2
Peeks La RH6 9 E2
Pegasus Ct RH11 14 D1
Pegasus Way RH19 21 F2
Pegler Way RH11 14 C2
Pegwell Cl RH11 14 C2
Pelham Ct,
Crawley RH11 15 E3

Pelham Ct,
Horsham RH12 36 C1
Pelham Dr RH11 14 D3
Pelham Pl,
Crawley RH11 15 E3
Pelham Pl,
Haywards Heath RH16 25 E4
Pembley Grn RH10 22 D6
Pembroke Rd RH10 12 C2
Pembury Cl RH10 27 F1
Pendean RH15 29 F6
Penfold Rd RH10 16 C3
Penhurst Cl*,
Lytton Dr RH10 13 E4
Penland Cl RH16 24 B4
Penland Rd RH16 24 B3
Penn Cl RH11 11 G2
Penn Cres RH16 25 E5
Pennine Cl RH11 11 E5
Peppard Rd RH10 16 D2
Pepper Dr RH15 28 C5
Percy Rd RH12 34 B6
Perimeter Rd East RH6 8 B2
Perimeter Rd North RH6 7 G1
Perimeter Rd South RH6 7 F5
Perkstead Ct*,
Gunning Cl RH11 14 D2
Perry Av RH19 20 D2
Perryfield Ho RH11 3 B4
Perryfield Rd RH11 3 A4
Perryfields RH15 28 C2
Perrylands RH6 6 C2
Perrymount Rd RH16 24 C6
Perth Cl RH11 11 G2
Perth Way RH12 35 F5
Peterborough Rd RH10 15 H3
Peterhouse Par RH10 12 C3
Peterlee Walk*,
Basildon Way RH11 14 B3
Petlands Gdns RH16 26 D1
Petlands Rd RH16 26 D1
Petworth Ct RH11 14 C2
Petworth Dr,
Burgess Hill RH15 29 E2
Petworth Dr,
Horsham RH12 35 F2
Pevensey Cl RH10 12 C6
Peverel Rd RH11 10 B6
Phillips Cl RH10 16 C4
Phoenix La RH19 22 C2
Pickers Grn RH16 25 E2
Pierpoint Cl BN6 30 D2
Pilgrim Ct RH16 25 E5
Pine Cl RH11 11 F2
Pine Gdns RH6 4 D5
Pine Gro RH10 20 A1
Pine Shaw RH10 12 D4
Pine Tree Cl BN6 31 F4
Pine Trees BN6 32 A2
Pine Way Cl RH19 20 D6
Pineham Copse RH16 24 D6
Pinehurst,
Burgess Hill RH15 29 E6
Pinehurst,
Horsham RH12 34 C5
Pinetops RH13 35 H5
Pinetrees Cl RH10 22 B5
Pinewood Cl RH12 38 B2
Pinewood Ct RH16 26 B3
Pinewood Way RH12 26 B3
Piries Pl RH12 36 D1
Pitt La BN6 31 E4
Plantain Cres RH11 14 D3
Playden Ct RH11 14 C3
Plough Cl RH11 10 C4
Plough La RH12 34 D5
Plover Cl RH11 11 F3
Plovers Rd RH13 35 F6
Poles La RH11 7 F5
Polestub La RH17 23 B2
Policemans La BN6 30 D3
Pollards RH11 10 D6
Pollards Dr RH13 37 F1
Pond Wood Rd RH10 12 B3
Pondcroft Rd RH16 24 B3
Pondside RH16 26 A1
Pondtail Cl RH11 34 D3
Pondtail Copse RH12 34 D3
Pondtail Dr RH12 34 D3
Pondtail Pl RH12 34 D3
Pondtail Rd RH12 34 C3
Poplar Cl RH11 11 F2
Poplar Mews RH16 26 A3
Portland Cl,
Burgess Hill RH15 28 C4
Portland Rd,
East Grinstead RH19 20 D5
Portsmouth La RH16 24 D2
Portsmouth Wood Rd RH16 24 D2
Portsmouth Wood Cl
RH16 24 D2
Potters Cft RH13 37 F1
Potters La RH15 28 D6

Potters Pl RH12 36 C
Pound Gate BN6 32 A
Pound Hill Pl RH10 12 D
Povey Cross Rd RH6 4 B
Poveys Cl RH16 28 B
Powell RH6 4 B
Poynes Rd RH6 4 B
Poynings Rd RH11 10 B
Prescott Gdns RH15 28 D
Prestwick Cl RH11 10 A
Prestwood Cl RH11 11 E
Prestwood Cl RH11 6 A
Priestcroft Cl RH11 10 D
Primrose Av RH6 5 E
Primrose Cl,
Burgess Hill RH15 28 B
Primrose Cl,
Crawley RH11 15 E
Primrose Copse RH12 34 D
Princess Rd RH11 3 A
Priors Walk RH10 3 E
Priory Cl RH6 4 C
Priory Rd,
Burgess Hill RH15 28 D
Priory Rd,
Hassocks BN6 32 B
Priory Way RH16 24 D
Proctor Dr RH10 16 C
Prospect Pl RH11 3 A
Pudding La RH6 6 B
Puffin Rd RH11 10 A
Punch Copse Rd RH10 12 C
Punnetts Ct RH11 14 C
Purcell Rd RH11 14 C
Purley Cl RH10 16 D
Purton Rd RH12 34 B
Pyecombe Ct RH11 14 C

Quail Cl RH12 34 D
Quakers La RH16 25 E
Quantock Cl RH11 11 E
Quarry Cl,
Burgess Hill RH15 29 G
Quarry Cl,
Horsham RH12 35 F
Quarry Hill RH16 24 A
Quarry Rise RH19 21 E
Quarterbrass Farm Rd
RH12 34 D
Queen Elizabeth Av
RH16 28 C
Queen St RH13 37 E
Queens Cres RH16 24 C
Queens Dr BN6 32 C
Queens Gate RH6 8 E
Queens Rd,
East Grinstead RH19 20 D
Queens Rd,
Haywards Heath RH16 24 C
Queens Rd, Horley RH6 4 D
Queens Sq RH10 3 D
Queens Walk RH19 20 D
Queens Way RH19 20 D
Queensway,
Crawley RH10 3 D
Queensway,
Horsham RH13 36 D
Questen Mews RH10 13 E

Racecourse Way RH6 4 B
Rackham Cl RH11 15 F
Radford Rd RH10 8 E
Railey Rd RH10 3 E
Railway Ap RH19 20 C
Rakers Ridge RH12 34 D
Raleigh Ct RH10 12 E
Raleigh Walk RH10 15 H
Ramblers Way RH11 15 E
Ramsey Cl, Horley RH6 4 C
Ramsey Cl,
Horsham RH12 34 D
Ramsey Ct RH11 14 C
Randall Scofield Ct*,
Crossways RH10 12 A
Randiddles Cl BN6 31 F
Ranmore Cl RH11 14 E
Ransome Cl RH11 14 E
Rastrick Cl RH11 15 E
Rathlin Rd RH11 15 E
Raven Cl RH12 34 D
Raven La RH11 11 A
Ravendene Ct RH11 3 C
Ravenscroft Ct RH12 34 C
Ravenswood BN6 32 C
Ravenswood Rd RH15 29 E
Raworth Ct RH10 16 C
Raymer Walk RH6 5 E
Reapers Cl RH12 34 D
Rectory La,
Crawley RH11 10 E
Rectory La, Horley RH6 6 E
Red Admiral St RH12 34 D

44

ed Deer Cl RH13 35 G6
Redditch Cl RH11 14 B3
Redford Av RH12 34 B5
Redgarth Ct RH19 20 A1
Redgrave Dr RH10 12 D6
Redkiln Cl RH13 35 E6
Redkiln Way RH13 35 E5
Redshank Ct*,
  Fairway RH11 14 A1
Redwing RH13 35 F6
Redwood Cl RH13 11 G3
Redwood Dr RH16 26 C2
Reed Pond Walk RH16 27 E1
Reedings RH11 14 A1
Reeds La RH16 30 A1
Regal Dr RH19 21 E5

Regent Bsns Pk RH15 28 B5

Regents Cl RH11 15 F3
Reigate Cl RH10 13 E3
Reigate Rd RH6 4 A4
Renfields RH16 26 A2
Reynard Cl RH12 35 G4
Reynolds Pl RH11 11 E4
Reynolds Rd RH11 11 E5
Rhodes Way RH10 15 H2
Rices Hill RH19 20 D4
Richardson Ct RH11 15 E4
Richborough Ct RH11 3 A2
Richmond Cl RH10 3 D4
Richmond Rd RH12 34 C6
Richmond Sq RH19 20 C2
Richmond Way RH19 21 E5
Rickfield RH11 10 D6
Rickwood RH6 5 E3
Ridge Way RH17 27 F2
Ridgehurst Dr RH12 36 A2
Ridgeside RH10 3 F2
Ridgeway,
  East Grinstead RH19 20 D5
Ridgeway,
  Horsham RH12 34 B5
Rillside RH10 16 A2
Rimmer Ct RH11 15 E5
Ring Rd North RH6 8 C2
Ring Rd South RH6 8 C2
Ringley Av RH6 4 D4
Ringley Oak RH12 35 E5
Ringley Rd RH12 35 E5
Ringwood Cl RH10 15 H1
Ritchie Cl RH10 16 C3
River Mead,
  Crawley RH11 10 D2
River Mead,
  Horsham RH12 36 B1
Riverside, Horley RH6 4 D6
Riverside,
  Horsham RH12 36 B1
Robert Way RH12 34 C6
Robin Cl, Crawley RH11 11 F3
Robin Cl,
  East Grinstead RH19 20 D3
Robin Hood La RH14 34 A4
Robin Rd RH15 28 A4
Robinson Ho RH11 3 B3
Robinswood Ct RH12 35 E5
Rocks La RH17 17 B6
Rocky La RH16 26 A4
Roebuck Cl RH10 35 G5
Roffey Cl RH6 4 C4
Roffeys Cl RH10 22 A5
Roffye Ct RH12 35 F5
Rolfe Dr RH15 29 G4
Romaine Cl RH15 29 G2
Rona Cl RH11 15 E2
Rook Way RH12 35 E3
Rookery Way RH16 36 A2
Rookwood Pk RH12 34 A6
Rookwood Way RH12 35 E2
Rosamund Rd RH10 16 B2
Rose Walk RH10 15 E1
Rosebarn Cl RH15 29 G6
Rosedale Cl RH11 14 D1
Rosemary Cl RH11 24 A5
Rosemary Ct RH6 4 B3
Rosemary La,
  Charlwood RH6 6 B2
Rosemary La,
  Horley RH6 5 E5
Rosemead Gdns RH10 3 D3
Roslan Ct RH6 5 E5
Ross Cl RH10 16 A2
Rossmore Cl RH10 13 E1
Rother Cres RH11 10 C6
Rothervale RH6 4 C1
Rothley Chase RH16 26 D1
Rough Fld RH19 20 C1
Rough Way RH12 35 F4
Roundway Ct*,
  London RH11 11 G3
Roundwood La RH16 24 D2
Rowan Cl, Crawley RH10 3 F2

Rowan Cl,
  Haywards Heath RH16 27 F1
Rowan Cl,
  Horsham RH12 35 H4
Rowan Walk RH10 18 D6
Rowan Way RH12 35 H4
Rowfant Cl RH10 13 E5
Rowlands Rd RH12 35 F3
Rowplatt La RH19 19 F2
Royal George Rd RH15 28 B3
Royce Rd RH10 12 A1
Royston Cl RH10 12 B2
Rudgwick Keep*,
  Langshott La RH6 5 G3
Rudgwick Rd RH11 10 C5
Rufwood RH10 18 B5
Rumbolds La RH16 26 B3
Runcorn Cl RH11 14 B3
Runshooke Ct RH11 14 D2
Rushams Rd RH12 34 B6
Rushetts Pl RH11 11 F2
Rushetts Rd RH11 11 E3
Rushhams Rd RH12 36 C1
Rushwood Cl RH11 27 F1
Ruskin Cl RH10 12 C3
Rusper Rd,
  Crawley RH11 10 A4
Rusper Rd,
  Horsham RH12 35 E5
Ruspers RH15 29 G5
Ruspers Keep RH11 10 C4
Russ Hill Rd RH6 6 A3
Russell Way RH10 12 A6
Russells Cres RH6 4 D5
Russet Cl RH6 5 F3
Rustlings Cl RH16 25 F5
Ruston Cl RH10 16 C2
Rutherford Way RH10 8 B6
Rutherwick Cl RH6 4 C4
Ruthven Ct RH17 23 B2
Rydal Cl RH11 14 A1
Ryders Way RH12 35 E2
Rye Ash RH10 12 B4
Ryecroft RH16 26 C1
Ryecroft Dr RH12 34 A6
Ryelands, Crawley RH11 10 D6
Ryelands, Horley RH6 5 E3

S

Sackville Cl RH19 20 B1
Sackville Ct RH19 21 E4
Sackville Gdns RH19 20 A2
Sackville La RH19 20 A2
Saddler Row RH10 15 G2
Saddlers Cl RH16 29 G6
Saffron Cl RH11 14 D3
St Agnes Rd RH19 20 C3
St Andrews Rd,
  Burgess Hill RH15 29 F3
St Andrews Rd,
  Crawley RH11 3 A2
St Annes Gdns BN6 32 D3
St Annes Rd RH16 27 F3
St Aubin Cl RH11 14 C3
St Barnabas Ct*,
  Crawley La RH10 12 C4
St Brelades Rd RH11 14 C3
St Catherines Rd RH10 12 D2
St Christophers Cl RH11 34 C5
St Christophers Rd BN6 31 E3
St Clement Rd RH11 14 C3
St Edmund Cl RH11 11 G2
St Edmunds Rd RH10 26 D1
St Edwards Cl RH19 20 D4
St Francis Cl RH16 26 D2
St Francis Gdns RH10 22 B5
St Francis Walk RH11 14 B1
St Georges Cl RH6 5 E4
St Georges Ct,
  Crawley RH10 11 G4
St Georges Ct,
  East Grinstead RH19 20 B2
St Georges Gdns RH13 35 E5
St Georges La BN6 31 F4
St Georges Pl BN6 31 F4
St Helier Cl RH11 14 C3
St Hildas Cl,
  Crawley RH11 14 D2
St Hildas Cl, Horley RH6 4 D3
St Hughs Cl RH10 12 D2
St James Rd RH19 20 C3
St James Walk RH11 15 F4
St Joan Cl RH11 11 G2
St Johns Av RH15 28 D4
St Johns Cl,
  East Grinstead RH19 20 D3
St Johns Cl,
  Horsham RH13 37 E2
St Johns Cres RH12 38 C2
St Johns Dr RH11 28 D4
St Johns Rd,
  Crawley RH11 3 A2
St Johns Rd,
  East Grinstead RH19 20 D3

St Johns Rd,
  Haywards Heath RH16 26 D2
St Josephs Way RH16 24 C6
St Lawrence Way BN6 31 E2
St Leonards Dr RH10 16 B2
St Leonards Pk RH19 20 A2
St Leonards Rd RH13 37 F3
St Margarets Rd RH19 21 E2
St Marks La RH12 35 E3
St Marys Dr RH10 12 C3
St Marys Gdns RH12 36 D2
St Marys Rd RH11 14 C3
St Marys Rd West RH15 28 C3
St Michaels Rd RH10 20 D3
St Nicholas Ct*,
  Crawley La RH10 12 C4
St Pauls Cl RH16 24 D5
St Peters Rd,
  Burgess Hill RH15 29 E3
St Peters Rd,
  Crawley RH11 3 A2
St Sampson Rd RH11 14 C3
St Stephen Cl RH11 11 G2
St Swithuns Cl RH19 21 E4
St Vincent Cl RH10 12 D6
St Wilfrids Rd RH11 14 B3
St Wilfrids Way RH16 24 C6
Salehurst Rd RH10 13 E5
Salisbury Rd,
  Crawley RH11 15 H4
Salisbury Rd,
  Horsham RH13 36 B4
Saltdean Cl RH11 15 F2
Salterns Rd RH10 16 C2
Salvington Rd RH11 14 C3
Samaritan Cl RH11 14 D3
Samphire Cl RH11 14 D3
San Feliu Ct RH19 21 F3
Sandeman Way RH13 37 F3
Sandhawes Hill RH19 21 F1
Sandhill La RH10 18 C6
Sandown St RH10 13 E5
Sandpiper Cl RH11 14 A1
Sandridge La RH16 24 D1
Sandringham Ct RH19 21 E5
Sandringham Rd RH11 15 E3
Sandrocks Way RH16 26 C2
Sandy La, Crawley RH10 18 B5
Sandy La,
  East Grinstead RH19 20 B2
Sandy Vale RH16 26 C2
Sandy Way RH16 26 C2
Sangers Dr RH6 4 C4
Sarel Way RH6 5 E2
Sargent Cl RH10 16 A3
Sark Cl RH11 14 D3
Saturn Cl RH11 14 B2
Saunders Ct RH10 12 D3
Savernake Walk RH10 16 A2
Savill Rd RH11 15 E2
Sawyers Cl RH15 29 G5
Saxby Rd RH15 28 B2
Saxley RH6 5 F3
Saxon Cres RH12 34 B5
Saxon Rd RH10 13 E6
Sayers Cl RH13 37 F1
Scallows Cl RH10 12 A4
Scallows Rd RH10 12 A4
Scamps Hill RH16 25 G4
Scholars Cl RH10 18 B6
School Cl,
  Burgess Hill RH15 28 D4
School Cl,
  Horsham RH12 35 G3
School La RH11 14 D2
Scory Cl RH11 14 D2
Scott Rd RH11 15 H2
Seaford Rd RH10 16 B3
Searles Vw RH12 35 E4
Seddon Ct*,
  Chippendale Rd RH11 15 E4
Sedgefield Rd RH11 15 E4
Sedgewick Cl RH10 13 E4
Sedgwick La RH13 37 G6
Selbourne Rd RH10 12 D2
Selby Cl RH16 26 C1
Selham Cl RH11 10 D5
Selsey Rd RH11 14 D4
Selwyn Cl RH10 12 D2
Semley Rd BN6 32 B2
Sequoia Pk RH11 15 F1
Sergison Cl RH16 24 B5
Sergison Rd RH16 24 B5
Serrin Way RH12 35 E4
Sevenfields RH15 28 A3
Severn Rd RH10 12 C6
Sewill Cl RH6 6 C2
Seymour Rd RH11 14 D3
Shackleton Rd RH10 16 B1
Shaftesbury Rd RH11 16 D1
Shandys Cl RH12 35 G4
Sharon Cl RH10 18 D5
Sharpthorne Cl RH11 15 E4
Sharrow Cl RH16 24 C6

Shaws Rd RH10 11 H4
Shearwater Ct*,
  Fairway RH11 14 A1
Sheddingdean Ct RH15 28 D2

Sheddingdean Ind Est RH15 28 D1

Sheffield Rd RH10 16 D1
Sheldon Cl RH10 16 D1
Shelley Cl RH10 12 C4
Shelley Ct RH16 24 C5
Shelley Dr RH12 38 B2
Shelley Rd,
  East Grinstead RH19 20 B4
Shelley Rd,
  Horsham RH12 34 B6
Shelley Wood RH15 28 A3
Shelleys Ct RH13 35 G6
Shenstone RH16 25 F2
Shepherd Cl RH10 15 G2
Shepherds Mead RH15 28 A3
Shepherds Walk BN6 32 B1
Shepherds Way RH12 35 G4
Sheppey Cl RH11 15 E3
Sheppeys RH16 26 B2
Sheridan Pl RH19 20 B4
Sherwood Dr RH16 24 A5
Sherwood Walk RH16 24 A5
Shetland Cl RH10 13 E4
Ship St RH19 20 D5
Shipley Bridge La RH10 9 F5
Shipley Rd RH11 10 C5
Shire Par RH10 13 E4
Shirley Cl RH11 14 B3
Shirleys BN6 33 G4
Shoreham Rd RH10 16 D2
Short Cl RH11 11 G3
Shorts Cl RH16 26 C1
Shortsfield Cl RH12 34 C4
Shottermill RH12 35 G2
Shotters RH11 28 C5
Sideways La RH6 4 A6
Silchester Dr RH11 15 E2
Silkin Walk RH11 15 E4
Silver Birches RH10 16 E4
Silver Cl RH10 25 E6
Silverdale BN6 32 D3
Silverdale Rd RH15 29 E5
Silverlea Gdns RH6 5 E4
Sinclair Cl RH10 16 C1
Singleton Rd RH12 38 B2
Singleton Way RH15 29 F6
Siskin Cl RH11 14 B3
Sissinghurst Cl RH10 16 D3
Skelmersdale Walk RH11 14 B3
Skipton Way RH6 5 E4
Skylark Vw RH12 34 D2
Slaugham Ct RH11 14 C2
Sleets Rd RH12 38 C2
Slimbridge Rd RH15 28 C3
Slinfold Walk RH11 10 D5
Sloughbrook Cl RH12 35 G4
Slugwash La RH17 27 F6
Smallfield Rd RH6 5 E4
Smallmead RH6 5 E4
Smalls La RH11 3 B2
Smalls Mead RH11 3 A2
Smalls Mead St RH11 14 D3
Smith Cl RH10 15 G2
Smithbarn RH13 37 G1
Smithbarn Cl RH6 5 E2
Smolletts RH19 20 B4
Snell Hatch RH11 11 E5
Snow Hill RH10 18 A1
Snow Hill La RH10 18 B1
Snowdrop Cl RH11 14 D3
Snowdrop La RH16 25 G6
Snowflakes La RH16 25 H4
Soane Cl RH11 14 B1
Somergate RH12 36 A1
Somerville Rd RH10 12 D3
Sorrel Cl RH11 14 D3
Sorrell Rd RH12 34 D4
South Av BN6 31 E4
South Bank BN6 32 A3
South Cl,
  Burgess Hill RH15 28 B3
South Cl, Crawley RH10 11 H4
South Dr RH15 28 B3
South Gro RH13 37 E2
South Holmes Rd RH13 35 H4
South Lodge Cl RH15 28 C2
South Parade RH6 4 C3
South Rd RH16 24 C6
South St, Hassocks BN6 33 F3
South St,
  Haywards Heath RH17 23 B4
South St,
  Haywards Heath RH16 26 C2
Southbrook RH11 15 F5
Southdown Cl,
  Horsham RH12 35 G4
Southgate Av RH10 3 D3
Southgate Rd RH10 15 G1

Southgate Rd RH10 15 G1
Southlands,
  East Grinstead RH19 20 C6
Southlands, Horley RH6 4 C4
Southlands Av RH6 4 C3
Southview BN6 33 G1
Southview RH10 18 A2
Southwark Cl*,
  Sandringham Rd RH11 15 E3
Southwater Cl RH10 10 D5
Southway,
  Burgess Hill RH15 28 B4
Southway, Horley RH6 8 C2
Southway RH10 20 C3

Sovereign Bsns Pk RH15 28 C5

Spanish Cl RH15 29 E3
Sparrow Way RH15 28 A4
Spatham La BN6 33 H4
Speedwell Way RH12 35 F4
Spencers Pl RH12 34 B5
Spencers Rd,
  Crawley RH11 3 A3
Spencers Rd,
  Horsham RH12 34 B6
Spicers Cl RH15 28 D2
Spiers Way RH6 5 E6
Spindle Way RH10 3 E3
Spinney Cl,
  Crawley RH11 18 D5
Spinney Cl,
  Hassocks BN6 31 F4
Spinney Cl,
  Horsham RH11 35 H3
Spooners Rd RH12 35 F5
Spring Cl RH11 3 B3
Spring Copse RH10 22 C5
Spring Gdns,
  Crawley RH11 22 C5
Spring Gdns,
  Horsham RH12 34 C6
Spring La,
  Haywards Heath RH16 25 F2
Spring Plat RH10 12 C5
Spring Way RH19 21 E1
Springfield RH10 12 A2
Springfield Cres RH12 36 C1
Springfield Ct,
  Crawley RH11 3 B3
Springfield Ct,
  Horsham RH12 36 D1
Springfield Park Rd RH12 36 C1
Springfield Pk RH12 34 C6
Springfield Rd,
  Crawley RH11 3 A3
Springfield Rd,
  Horsham RH12 36 C1
Spurgeon Cl RH11 3 A1
Squires Cl RH10 18 B5
Squirrel Cl RH11 11 E2
Stable Cl RH10 16 D2
Stace Way RH10 13 E3
Stackfield Rd RH11 14 B1
Stafford Rd RH11 10 D2
Stafford Way RH6 32 C3
Staffords Pl RH6 5 E5
Stagelands RH11 11 E3
Stan Hill RH6 6 A1
Stanbridge Cl RH11 10 B6
Stander Cl RH19 19 H2
Standen Pl RH12 35 F2
Stanford Av BN6 32 A2
Stanford Cl BN6 32 A2
Stanford Ct RH10 16 D1
Stanford Ter RH10 32 B2
Stanford Way RH12 38 B2
Stanier Cl RH10 12 A2

Stanley Centre RH10 12 A2

Stanley Cl RH10 15 H2
Stanley Walk RH13 37 E2
Stans Way RH12 36 D2
Staplecross Ct RH11 14 C3
Staplefield Rd RH17 23 A1
Star Cl RH13 35 F5
Starleys BN6 30 B3
Starling Cl RH15 28 A4
Station App,
  Hassocks BN6 32 B2
Station App, Horley RH6 5 E4
Station Approach Rd
  RH6 8 B1
Station Cl RH13 37 E1
Station Cotts BN6 32 B2
Station Hill RH10 12 C5
Station Rd,
  Burgess Hill RH15 28 B3
Station Rd,
  Crawley RH11 3 C3
Station Rd,
  Crawley Down RH10 18 C5

45

Station Rd,
East Grinstead RH19 20 C4
Station Rd, Horley RH6 5 E4
Station Rd,
Horsham RH13 37 E1
Station Rd,
Warnham RH12 34 A1
Station Way RH10 3 C3
Steers La RH10 8 C5
Stephenson Dr RH19 20 D6
Stephenson Pl RH10 12 B6
Stephenson Way RH10 14 B3
Stevenage Rd RH11 14 B3
Steyning Cl RH11 11 H3
Stirling Cl,
Burgess Hill RH15 29 F2
Stirling Cl,
Crawley RH10 16 C1
Stirling Court Rd RH15 29 F2
Stirling Way,
East Grinstead RH19 21 F1
Stirling Way,
Horsham RH13 37 F1
Stirrup Way RH10 13 E4
Stockcroft Rd RH17 17 C5
Stockfield RH6 5 E3
Stocklands Cl RH17 23 C2
Stocks Cl RH6 5 E5
Stockwell Ct RH16 26 C1
Stokers Cl RH6 7 G1
Stokes Cl RH10 16 D2
Stonebridge Ct RH12 36 C2
Stonecourt Cl RH6 5 F4
Stonecrop Cl RH11 14 D2
Stonefield Cl RH11 3 C4
Stonefield Way RH15 28 D2
Stoneleigh Cl RH19 21 E3
Stonepound Rd BN6 32 A2
Stoneybrook RH12 36 A2
Stoneycroft Walk*,
Fairway RH11 14 A1
Stopham Rd RH10 16 D2
Storrington Ct RH11 10 D4
Strand Cl RH10 16 D2
Strathfield Cl RH16 26 D1
Strathmore Rd RH11 10 D2
Stream Pk RH19 19 H2
Street Hill RH10 13 E6
Strickland Cl RH11 10 B6
Stroudley Cl RH10 12 C6
Strudgate Cl RH10 16 B1
Stuart Cl RH10 12 D6
Stuart Way RH19 21 E5
Stubfield RH12 34 A6
Stumblemead RH17 17 C6
Stumblets RH10 12 D4
Suffolk Cl RH6 4 D5
Sugworth Cl RH16 24 B3
Sullington Hill RH11 15 F1
Sullington Mead RH12 38 C2
Sullivan Dr RH11 14 B3
Summer Ho RH11 3 B2
Summerhill RH16 24 D4
Summerhill Dr RH16 25 E3
Summerhill Grange
RH16 24 D3
Summerhill La RH16 24 D3
Summersvere Ct RH10 12 B2
Sundew Cl RH11 14 D3
Sunningdale Ct RH11 3 B4
Sunny Av RH10 18 B6
Sunnyhill Cl RH10 18 C5
Sunnymead,
Crawley RH11 3 B2
Sunnymead,
Crawley Down RH10 18 C5
Sunnywood Dr RH16 26 B2
Sunset La RH15 29 E6
Sunte Av RH16 24 D3
Sunte Cl RH16 24 C3
Surrey Ct*,
New St RH13 37 E2
Sussex Border Path RH6 6 A4
Sussex Ct RH16 26 C1
Sussex Gdns RH17 27 F2
Sussex Lodge RH12 34 C5
Sussex Manor
Bsns Pk RH10 12 A1
Sussex Rd RH16 26 D1
Sussex Sq RH16 26 C1
Sussex Way RH15 28 B3
Swaledale Cl RH16 15 E2
Swallow Rd RH11 11 F3
Swallow Rest RH15 28 A3
Swallowtail Rd RH12 35 E3
Swan La RH6 6 C2
Swan Sq RH12 36 D1
Swan Walk RH12 36 D1
Swan Yd RH12 36 D1
Swann Cl RH15 29 G3
Swann Way RH12 38 C2
Sweetlands BN6 32 D1

Swift Cl RH15 28 A3
Swift La RH11 11 F3
Swindon Rd RH12 34 B5
Sycamore Av RH12 35 H4
Sycamore Cl RH11 11 F2
Sycamore Dr RH19 21 F4
Sydney Rd RH16 24 C5
Sylvan Cl RH16 27 F1
Sylvan Rd RH10 16 A1
Syresham Gdns RH16 26 D1

Tallis Cl RH11 14 C2
Talman Cl RH11 14 B1
Tamar Cl RH10 12 C6
Tanbridge Pk RH12 36 C2
Tanbridge Pl RH12 36 C2
Tanfield Ct RH12 36 C1
Tangle Oak RH19 19 F1
Tangmere Rd RH11 10 C5
Tanners Cross RH16 26 A2
Tanyard Av RH19 21 E5
Tanyard Cl,
Crawley RH10 16 C2
Tanyard Cl,
Horsham RH13 37 E2
Tanyard Way RH6 5 E2
Tarham Cl RH6 4 B2
Tate Cres RH15 28 D3
Tatham Ct*,
Chippendale Rd RH11 15 E4
Taunton Cl RH10 13 E5
Taylor Walk RH11 3 A1
Teal Cl RH12 34 C4
Teasel Cl RH11 15 E3
Teesdale RH11 15 F2
Telford Pl RH10 3 E3
Telham Ct RH11 14 C2
Temple Cl RH10 12 D6
Temple Gro RH15 28 B3
Tennyson Cl,
Crawley RH10 12 C3
Tennyson Cl,
Horsham RH12 35 E3
Tennyson Ct RH16 24 D5
Tennyson Rise RH19 20 B4
Tern Rd RH11 10 A6
Terry Rd RH11 15 E5
Thatcher Ct RH10 15 G2
Thatchers Cl,
Burgess Hill RH15 29 G6
Thatchers Cl,
Horley RH6 5 E2
Thatchers Cl,
Horsham RH12 34 D5
The Acorns,
Burgess Hill RH15 28 A2
The Acorns,
Crawley RH11 15 E5
The Avenue,
Crawley RH10 15 G4
The Avenue, Horley RH6 4 C5
The Belfry RH19 20 C4
The Birches RH10 12 B4
The Blackthorns RH15 29 F2
The Blytons RH19 20 A4
The Boulevard RH10 3 C2
The Bourne BN6 32 B1
The Bower,
Crawley RH10 12 C6
The Bower,
Haywards Heath RH16 24 B6
The Brambles RH17 23 C3
The Broadway,
Crawley RH10 3 C2
The Broadway,
Haywards Heath RH16 24 C5
The Brontes RH19 20 C4
The Brook RH10 11 G4
The Brooks RH15 28 C2
The Brow RH15 28 D4
The Brownings*,
Garden Wood Rd RH19 20 E4
The Cackstones RH10 13 E4
The Canter RH10 13 E4
The Castle RH12 35 E2
The Causeway RH12 36 D2
The Cedars RH16 24 B3
The Chase RH10 16 A1
The Chestnuts RH10 3 C3
The Close,
Burgess Hill RH15 29 G3
The Close,
East Grinstead RH19 20 B5
The Close,
Hassocks BN6 32 C2
The Close, Horley RH6 5 F6
The Coppice RH10 18 D5
The Copse,
Haywards Heath RH16 24 B5
The Copse,
Crawley RH10 12 A5
The Coronet RH6 5 F6
The Courtyard,
Crawley RH10 3 C3

The Courtyard,
East Grinstead RH19 21 F4
The Covey RH10 13 E3
The Crescent,
Hassocks BN6 32 D3
The Crescent,
Horley RH6 4 D6
The Crescent,
Horsham RH12 36 B2
The Croft, Crawley RH11 10 D6
The Croft,
Hassocks BN6 32 B1
The Dakins RH19 20 D5
The Dell,
Haywards Heath RH16 24 B5
The Dell, Horley RH6 5 F6
The Dingle RH11 11 E5
The Driftway RH11 3 B1
The Drive,
Burgess Hill RH15 29 E3
The Drive,
Crawley RH10 22 C5
The Drive,
Haywards Heath RH16 24 D2
The Drive, Horley RH6 5 E5
The Drove BN6 33 F3
The Droveway RH16 24 A5
The Dymocks BN6 33 F3
The Felbridge
Centre RH19 19 H2
The Feld RH19 19 H2
The Fieldings RH6 5 F2
The Foresters RH13 37 G3
The Forge RH6 6 B2
The Gables,
Crawley RH10 22 B6
The Gables,
Horsham RH12 34 C5
The Garrones RH10 13 E4
The Gattons RH15 28 B3
The Gilligans RH15 28 C2
The Glade,
Crawley RH10 16 A1
The Glade,
Horsham RH13 35 G6
The Glades RH19 21 G4
The Glebe,
Crawley RH10 22 B5
The Glebe,
East Grinstead RH19 19 H1
The Glebe,
Hassocks BN6 31 E3
The Glebe,
Haywards Heath RH16 25 E3
The Glebe, Horley RH6 4 C4
The Grange RH6 4 D1
The Green,
Copthorne RH10 22 B5
The Green,
Crawley RH11 11 F5
The Grooms RH10 13 E4
The Grove,
Crawley RH11 11 F5
The Grove,
Haywards Heath RH16 27 F1
The Grove, Horley RH6 5 E5
The Ham BN6 31 H5
The Hawthorns RH16 29 E2
The Highlands RH17 23 C1
The Hollands RH15 29 F3
The Hollow,
Crawley RH11 10 C6
The Hollow,
Haywards Heath RH16 25 F6
The Holt RH15 29 G5
The Hornbeams RH15 28 A2
The Jays RH10 28 C3
The Jordans RH10 20 D5
The Kiln RH15 29 G3
The Knowle RH17 23 B2
The Larches,
East Grinstead RH19 21 F1
The Larches,
Horsham RH16 35 H3
The Laurels RH16 24 A6
The Leas RH15 28 C3
The Limes RH19 19 H1
The Lindens RH10 22 B5
The Link RH11 3 B1
The Maltings RH15 28 A3
The Mardens RH11 11 E4
The Marlings RH16 26 A2
The Martins RH10 19 E5
The Martlets*,
Burgess Hill RH15 29 E4
The Martlets,
Crawley RH10 3 D2
The Meadow RH10 22 A5
The Meadows BN6 32 B1
The Meads RH19 20 D6
The Meadway RH6 5 F4
The Mews RH12 38 B1
The Millbank RH11 10 C6
The Minnels BN6 32 C1

The Moorings RH19 19 H2
The Nurseries RH19 17 C5
The Nursery RH15 29 F3
The Oaks,
Burgess Hill RH15 28 A2
The Oaks,
East Grinstead RH19 21 F4
The Oaks,
Haywards Heath RH16 25 F6
The Orchard BN6 32 B3
The Orchard RH13 35 H5
The Orchards,
Broadbridge Heath
RH12 38 B2
The Orchards,
Crawley RH11 14 A1
The Orchards,
Haywards Heath RH16 24 C6
The Orchards,
Horsham RH12 35 F4
The Paddock,
Crawley RH10 13 E4
The Paddock,
Horsham RH12 38 C2
The Paddocks RH16 26 A1
The Parade RH10 11 H4
The Pasture RH10 12 C6
The Pavement RH10 3 D2
The Pines,
Crawley RH10 12 D5
The Pines,
Haywards Heath RH16 25 F6
The Pines,
Horsham RH12 35 H4
The Plat RH12 36 B1
The Platt RH16 25 F5
The Poplars,
Hassocks BN6 32 C3
The Poplars,
Horsham RH13 37 F1
The Pound RH15 28 D2
The Quadrant BN6 32 D2
The Ridgeway,
Burgess Hill RH15 29 E2
The Ridgeway,
Horley RH6 4 D6
The Ridings,
Burgess Hill RH15 29 F5
The Ridings,
Crawley RH10 13 E4
The Rise, Crawley RH10 12 D5
The Rise,
East Grinstead RH19 20 D5
The Rise,
Haywards Heath RH16 25 F6
The Rocks RH19 22 B2
The Rowans RH15 28 A2
The Rushes RH15 27 G1
The Saffrons RH15 28 C2
The Satellite
Bsns Village RH10 11 H1
The Sayers RH19 20 B4
The Spinney,
Burgess Hill RH15 29 E2
The Spinney,
Crawley RH11 15 E1
The Spinney,
Hassocks BN6 32 B1
The Spinney,
Haywards Heath RH16 24 B3
The Spinney,
Horley RH6 4 D2
The Square RH10 3 C2
The Stennings RH19 20 B2
The Street,
Albourne BN6 30 B3
The Street,
Ditchling BN6 33 H6
The Street, Horley RH6 6 B2
The Twitten,
Burgess Hill RH15 29 E2
The Twitten,
Crawley RH11 11 E5
The Twitten,
Ditchling BN6 33 F3
The Twitten,
Hassocks BN6 30 B3
The Vineries RH15 29 G3
The Warren RH15 29 F5
The Weald RH19 21 E1
The Welkin RH16 25 F2
The Wickets RH15 28 C2
The Wilderness RH15 25 F2
The Willows,
Burgess Hill RH15 29 F1
The Willows,
Horsham RH12 34 C4
Thelton Av RH12 38 B2
Theobalds Rd,
Burgess Hill RH15 26 B6
Theobalds Rd,
Burgess Hill RH15 29 F1
Thetford Walk RH11 14 B3
Theydon Cl RH10 16 A1

Thirlmere Rd RH11 14 A
Thompson Ct*,
Chadwick Cl RH11 15 E
Thorndyke Cl RH10 16 D
Thornhill RH11 15 E
Thornhurst RH15 29 G
Thornton Cl RH6 4 B
Thornton Pl RH6 4 B
Three Acres RH12 36 B
Three Bridges Rd RH10 3 F
Ticehurst Cl RH10 13 F
Tilers Cl RH15 29 G
Tilgate Dr,
Crawley RH10 15 G
Tilgate Dr,
Crawley RH10 15 G
Tilgate Forest
Bsns Centre RH11 15 F
Tilgate Par RH10 15 H
Tilgate Pl RH10 15 H
Tilgate Way RH10 15 H
Tillotson Cl RH10 12 D
Tiltwood Dr RH10 18 D
Timber Ct RH12 34 C
Timberham Farm Rd
RH6 7 G
Timberham Way RH6 7 G
Timberlands RH11 15 E
Tindal Cl RH15 29 G
Tinsley Cl RH10 12 B
Tinsley Grn RH10 8 C
Tinsley La RH10 12 B
Tinsley La North RH10 8 C
Tinsley La South RH10 12 B
Tintern Rd RH11 14 D
Tiree Path RH11 15 E
Titchfield Cl RH15 29 G
Tithe Orch RH19 19 F
Titmus Dr RH10 15 H
Todds Cl RH6 4 C
Toftwood Cl RH10 12 D
Tollgate RH16 25 F
Tollgate Hill RH11 15 E
Tollgate La RH17 23 B
Tott Hill BN6 31 F
Tower Cl,
East Grinstead RH19 20 C
Tower Cl, Horley RH6 4 C
Tower Cl,
Horsham RH13 36 B
Tower Ct*,
Tower Cl RH19 20 D
Tower Hill RH13 36 B
Tower House Cl RH17 23 B
Town Barn Rd RH11 3 B
Town Ct RH11 3 B
Town Mead RH11 3 B
Trafalgar Rd RH12 34 B
Treadcroft Dr RH12 35 E
Treeview RH11 15 E
Trefoil Cl RH12 35 E
Trefoil Cres RH11 14 D
Trenear Cl RH13 37 F
Trent Cl RH11 14 C
Trevanne Plat RH10 12 D
Trevelyn Pl RH16 24 C
Trewaren Ct RH11 11 E
Treyford Cl RH11 10 C
Triangle Rd RH16 26 D
Triangle Way RH15 28 A
Trinity Cl RH10 12 D
Trinity Ct, Hassocks BN6 31 F
Trinity Ct,
Horsham RH12 34 C
Trinity Rd BN6 31 E
Trinity Sq RH13 37 E
Troon Cl RH11 10 A
Trotton Cl RH10 16 C
Troymede RH17 17 C
Trundle Mead RH12 34 C
Tudor Cl,
East Grinstead RH19 21 E
Tudor Gdns RH15 28 D
Tulip Ct RH12 34 C
Tullett Rd RH10 16 C
Tunnmeade*,
Fairway RH11 15 E
Turkey La RH15 29 E
Turner Cl RH19 21 F
Turner Walk RH10 16 A
Turners Hill Rd,
Crawley RH10 13 E
Turners Hill Rd,
Crawley Down RH10 18 A
Turners Hill Rd,
East Grinstead RH19 20 A
Turners Mill Cl RH16 24 B
Turners Mill Rd RH16 24 B
Turners Way RH15 28 C
Turnpike RH11 11 G
Turret Cl*,
Buckhurst Way RH19 20 C
Tuscany Gdns RH10 11 G

46

Entry	Ref
shmore Av RH10	11 G2
shmore Cres RH10	11 G3
shmore Ct RH10	11 G3
xford Ct RH10	11 G3
ssock CI RH11	14 D1
xford CI RH10	16 C1
eed La RH10	10 C3
tten La RH19	19 F2
o Mile Ash RH13	36 A5
yhurst Ct RH19	20 C2
yne CI RH11	14 C2
yner CI RH6	5 F3
den Way RH12	35 F3
er Rd RH10	15 G2
ers Grn RH17	23 D5
mperley Ct RH13	35 E6
ne CI RH10	16 D1
derhill La BN6	32 A5
derwood CI RH10	18 D5
field RH6	4 D5
field CI RH6	4 D6
park Gdns RH12	35 F3
per Beacon Rd BN6	33 F6
per Forecourt RH6	8 C2
per St Johns Rd r15	28 D3
per Stables RH16	26 A1
town Hill RH16	26 A2
le Dr RH12	36 C1
e Rd RH14	26 C3
ebridge CI RH15	29 F1
ebridge Dr RH15	29 F1
ebridge Rd RH15	29 F2
entine Dr RH15	28 B3
lance CI RH15	28 B2
nbrugh CI RH11	14 B2
ncouver Dr RH11	11 G2
nners RH10	11 G4
rbania Way RH19	21 F3
non CI RH12	35 F5
arage La RH6	4 C3
arage Rd RH10	18 B6
toria Av RH15	28 B4
toria CI, urgess Hill RH15	28 C4
toria CI, Horley RH6	4 D4
toria CI RH13	37 E2
toria Way RH15	28 C4
ctoria Ind Est, urgess Hill RH15	**28 A4**
ctoria Ind Est, urgess Hill RH15	**28 C5**
toria Mews RH11	3 B2
toria Rd, alcombe RH17	17 C5
toria Rd, urgess Hill RH15	28 B4
toria Rd, rawley RH11	3 A2
toria Rd, aywards Heath RH16	27 E1
toria Rd, Horley RH6	4 D4
toria St RH13	37 E2
toria Way, urgess Hill RH15	28 C4
toria Way, aywards Heath RH16	21 E6
ctory Rd RH12	34 B6
ews Path RH16	27 F1
all Gdns RH12	38 B1
cent CI RH13	37 F2
rienne CI RH11	11 G2
can CI RH11	15 F3
iddington CI RH11	14 D2
dham CI RH10	12 C2
egg CI RH19	21 E4
agtail CI RH12	34 C2
ain End RH12	34 D4
ainwrights RH11	15 F2
akehams Grn Dr RH12	13 E2
akehurst Dr RH10	15 F2
akehurst Mews RH12	36 A2
akefield Ct RH12	36 C1
aldby Ct*,	
evile CI RH11	14 D2
alesbeech RH10	12 B6
alker Rd RH10	16 C1
all Hill Rd RH19	22 C3
allis Way,	
urgess Hill RH15	28 B2
allis Way,	
orsham RH13	35 G5
alnut Ct RH13	37 F2
Walnut La RH11	11 E2
Walnut Pk RH16	27 F1
Waltersville Way RH6	5 F6
Walton Dr RH13	35 H5
Walton Heath RH10	13 E3
Wandle CI RH10	16 C1
Wantage CI RH10	16 C2
Warburton CI RH19	21 F4
Warden Ct RH17	23 C4
Ware Ct RH15	29 G3
Warelands RH15	28 C5
Warner CI RH10	16 C3
Warner Ct RH15	28 D4
Warnham Rd, Broadbridge Heath RH12	38 B2
Warnham Rd, Crawley RH10	16 B2
Warnham Rd, Horsham RH12	34 B4
Warren CI RH19	19 G2
Warren Dr RH11	10 D4
Warrington CI RH11	14 B3
Washington Rd, Crawley RH11	14 B3
Washington Rd, Haywards Heath RH16	25 E5
Wassand CI RH10	12 B5
Water Lea RH10	16 B1
Water Vw*, Grays Wood RH6	5 F4
Watercress RH13	35 F6
Waterfield CI RH13	37 F1
Waterfield Gdns RH11	14 C3
Waterside, East Grinstead RH19	21 F4
Waterside, Horley RH6	4 D2
Waterside CI RH11	16 C2
Watson CI RH10	16 C2
Waveney Walk*, Norwich Rd RH10	16 B1
Waverley Ct RH12	36 C1
Wayside RH11	14 B1
Weald CI, Hassocks BN6	30 D2
Weald CI, Horsham RH13	37 E3
Weald Dr RH10	12 A6
Weald Rd RH15	28 B3
Weald Rise RH16	26 D4
Wealden Way RH16	24 B6
Weaver CI RH11	14 B1
Weavers CI RH15	29 G5
Webb CI RH11	15 E4
Weddell Rd RH10	15 H2
Weirbrook RH10	16 A2
Welbeck CI RH15	29 G2
Welbeck Dr RH15	29 G2
Wellcroft Cotts BN6	30 A3
Weller CI RH10	13 E6
Wellfield RH19	22 A1
Wellington CI RH10	13 E2
Wellington Rd RH12	37 E1
Wellington Town Rd RH19	20 C2
Wellington Way RH6	4 C2
Wells CI RH12	36 A1
Wells Lea RH19	20 C1
Wells Mdw RH19	20 C1
Wells Rd RH10	15 H3
Wellwood CI RH12	35 G5
Welwyn CI RH11	14 B3
Wenlock CI RH11	14 D1
Wensleydale RH11	15 F2
Wentworth Dr RH10	12 D4
Wesley CI, Crawley RH11	14 B2
Wesley CI, Horley RH6	4 D2
West Av RH10	12 A4
West Common RH16	24 D4
West Common Dr RH16	25 E4
West Furlong CI BN6	31 E3
West Furlong La BN6	31 E3
West Green Dr RH11	3 A1
West Hill RH19	20 C5
West Hill Dr RH15	28 C4
West Hill Walk RH15	28 C4
West La RH10	20 C5
West Leigh RH19	20 D5
West Mallions RH16	27 E2
West Par RH12	34 C5
West Park Cres RH15	28 B3
West Park Rd RH10	18 A2
West St, Burgess Hill RH15	28 B3
West St, Crawley RH11	3 B3
West St, East Grinstead RH19	20 D4
West St, Hassocks BN6	33 F3
West St, Horsham RH12	36 C1
West View Cotts RH16	25 F4
West View Gdns RH19	20 D4
West View Rd RH16	25 F4
West Way RH10	12 A5
Westcott CI RH11	15 F5
Westcott Keep*, Langshott La RH6	5 E3
Western Rd, Burgess Hill RH15	28 C3
Western Rd, Hassocks BN6	30 D2
Western Rd, Haywards Heath RH16	26 D1
Westfield Rd RH11	11 E6
Westlands Rd RH16	25 F5
Westleas RH6	4 B2
Westminster Rd RH10	12 C6
Westons CI RH12	34 D2
Westup Rd RH17	17 A5
Westway, Crawley RH10	9 G6
Westway, Horley RH6	8 C2
Wheatfield Way RH6	5 E2
Wheatsheaf CI, Burgess Hill RH15	28 B2
Wheatsheaf CI, Horsham RH12	35 E4
Wheatsheaf La RH17	23 C3
Wheatstone CI RH10	8 B6
Wheeler CI RH16	26 D2
Wheeler Rd RH10	16 C1
Wheelers Way RH19	19 F2
Wheelwright La RH15	29 G5
Whistler CI RH10	16 A2
White Hart CI RH12	34 C5
White Horse Rd RH12	35 G3
Whitecroft RH6	5 E3
Whitehall Pl RH11	10 B6
Whitemans CI RH17	23 B1
Whitemans Grn RH17	23 A2
Whites CI RH16	21 E2
Whitgift Walk RH10	15 G2
Whitmore Way RH6	4 B3
Whittington Rd RH10	15 G2
Whittle Way RH10	8 B5
Whitworth Rd RH11	11 G1
Whyteleaf Ho RH10	12 B5
Wickham CI, Haywards Heath RH16	24 C4
Wickham CI, Horley RH6	4 C3
Wickham Dr BN6	31 G4
Wickham Hill BN6	31 F4
Wickham Way RH16	24 C3
Wickhurst Gdns RH12	38 C2
Wickhurst La RH12	38 C2
Wickland Ct RH10	15 G2
Widgeon Way RH12	34 C4
Wilberforce CI RH11	15 E5
Wilderness Rd RH16	21 E2
Wildgoose Dr RH12	38 D2
Wildwood Rd RH12	38 D3
Wilkinson Ct RH11	15 E4
William Allen La RH16	25 F5
William Morris Way RH11	15 E5
Williams Way RH10	12 B5
Willow Brean RH6	4 B3
Willow CI, Crawley RH10	11 H3
Willow CI, East Grinstead RH19	20 C2
Willow CI, Hassocks BN6	31 E2
Willow Corner RH6	6 C2
Willow Gdns BN6	31 E1
Willow Mead RH19	21 E5
Willow Pk RH16	25 F6
Willow Rd RH12	35 G4
Willow Way RH6	31 E1
Willowfield RH11	3 B4
Willowrook Way BN6	32 C3
Wilmington CI, Crawley RH11	15 E5
Wilmington CI, Hassocks BN6	32 C2
Wilmington Way RH15	25 E5
Wilson CI RH10	16 D2
Wilton Villas RH17	17 C5
Wimblehurst Rd RH12	34 C5
Wincanton CI RH10	13 E5
Winchester Rd RH10	15 G3
Windermere Rd RH16	24 D6
Windmill Av BN6	32 C3
Windmill CI, Horley RH6	5 E4
Windmill CI, Horsham RH13	35 F6
Windmill Ct RH11	11 G3
Windmill Dr RH15	29 E3
Windmill La, Ashurst Wood RH19	22 A2
Windmill La, East Grinstead RH19	20 C1
Windrum CI RH12	36 A3
Windrush CI RH11	14 C1
Windsor CI, Crawley RH11	15 F3
Windsor CI, Haywards Heath RH16	26 C2
Windsor Pl RH19	21 E5
Windy Ridge RH11	10 D6
Wingle Tye Rd RH15	28 D6
Winkfield Ct RH16	24 C5
Winkhurst Way RH15	29 G6
Winnals Pk RH16	24 B5
Winners Way RH6	7 F2
Winterbourne RH12	35 F2
Winter Gdns RH13	3 A4
Winterfold RH10	16 A2
Winterton Ct RH13	37 E1
Wisborough Ct*, Cowfold CI RH11	14 C1
Wisden Av RH15	28 C2
Wiston Ct RH11	14 C2
Wither Dale RH6	4 B2
Withey Brook RH6	4 B6
Withey Mdws RH6	4 A6
Withy Bush RH15	28 B2
Wivelsfield Rd RH16	26 D2
Woburn Rd RH11	14 D1
Wold CI RH11	14 C1
Woldhurstlea CI RH11	14 D1
Wolstonbury CI, Crawley RH11	15 F1
Wolstonbury CI, Hassocks BN6	31 F4
Wolstonbury Ct RH15	29 E4
Wolstonbury Way RH15	29 E4
Wolverton CI RH6	4 C6
Wolverton Gdns RH6	4 C5
Wood End RH10	35 H4
Wood Ride RH16	26 C2
Wood St RH19	20 C4
Woodbanke La RH16	26 A2
Woodbridge Ct RH12	35 F5
Woodbury Av RH19	21 F3
Woodbury Ct RH19	21 F5
Woodcote RH6	5 E3
Woodcourt RH11	15 F4
Woodcrest Rd RH15	28 D6
Woodcroft RH15	28 D2
Woodcroft Rd RH11	14 A1
Woodend CI RH10	12 B3
Woodfield CI RH10	11 H4
Woodfield Rd RH10	3 E1
Woodgates CI RH13	37 F1
Woodhall RH17	23 B2
Woodhayes RH6	5 E3
Wooding Gro RH11	15 E5
Woodland Av RH15	29 F3
Woodland CI, Burgess Hill RH15	29 F3
Woodland CI, Horsham RH13	35 G5
Woodland Cres RH15	29 F3
Woodland Dr RH10	18 D6
Woodland Way RH13	35 G5
Woodlands, Crawley RH10	12 D3
Woodlands, Horley RH6	5 F3
Woodlands CI RH10	18 D6
Woodlands Rd, East Grinstead RH19	21 E1
Woodlands Rd, Haywards Heath RH16	24 D6
Woodleigh Rd RH15	29 F2
Woodmans Hill RH11	15 F4
Woodpecker Cres RH15	28 A4
Woodridge Dr RH16	27 E1
Woodroyd Av RH6	4 C5
Woodroyd Gdns RH6	4 C6
Woods Hill CI RH19	22 B2
Woods Hill La RH19	22 B2
Woodside RH13	35 G6
Woodside Rd RH10	12 A3
Woodsland CI RH15	32 B2
Woodsland Rd BN6	32 B2
Woodstock RH19	20 B3
Woodstock CI RH12	34 D4
Woodwards RH11	15 E4
Woodwards CI RH15	29 F6
Woolborough CI RH10	11 G4
Woolborough La RH10	12 A2
Woolborough Rd RH10	11 G4
Woolven CI RH15	28 C6
Worcester Rd RH10	15 H3
Wordsworth CI RH10	12 C4
Wordsworth Pl RH12	35 E2
Wordsworth Rise RH19	20 B4
Worsted La RH19	21 G5
Worth Ct RH10	12 D5
Worth Park Av RH10	12 C4
Worth Rd RH10	12 C5
Worth Way RH10	13 E6
Worthing Rd RH12	36 B6
Wray CI RH19	22 B2
Wren CI, Burgess Hill RH15	28 A4
Wren CI, Horsham RH12	34 D2
Wren Ct RH10	15 H2
Wright CI RH10	16 C4
Wroxham Walk*, Norwich Rd RH10	16 B1
Wyberlye Rd RH15	28 D3
Wychperry Rd RH16	24 B5
Wycliffe Ct*, Booth Rd RH11	14 B3
Wye CI RH11	15 F5
Wykeham Way RH15	29 F5
Wynlea CI RH10	18 B6
Wysemead RH6	5 F3
Wythwood RH16	26 D3
Wyvern Way RH11	29 F3
Yale Dr RH12	34 B6
Yarmouth CI RH10	16 B1
Yarrow Ct RH12	34 D4
Yattendon Rd RH6	5 E4
Yew La RH19	20 A2
Yew Tree CI RH6	4 D3
Yew Tree Ct RH17	23 C3
Yew Tree Rd RH6	6 B2
Yewlands Walk*, Fairway RH11	14 A1
York Av RH19	21 E5
York CI RH13	35 F6
York Rd, Burgess Hill RH15	28 A4
York Rd, Crawley RH10	15 H3